D0469484

1

The Science of Likability: 27 Studies to Master Charisma, Attract Friends, Captivate People, and Take Advantage of Human Psychology

By Patrick King
Social Interaction and Conversation Coach at
www.PatrickKingConsulting.com

Table of Contents

Introduction

Like many college underclassmen who had no idea what they wanted to study, I chose to major in psychology.

I thought it was a good default choice because the knowledge theoretically had wide application and could transfer to any other field. After all, psychology is the study of why people act in specific ways, and I would be dealing with *people* anywhere I went, right? It also didn't hurt that I heard the vast majority of the classes had open-book, multiple-choice midterms and finals.

So I checked the box next to "Bachelor of

Science in Psychology" and went on with my day. It was originally a shot in the dark, but in reality, I could have done much worse; psychology has turned out to be incredibly applicable to my life and career.

The study of psychology isn't about reading minds or interpreting dreams, though I had a fair number of people asking about that. It's simply the study of *why people do the things they do*.

There were the obvious applications, such as discovering exactly what works in advertisements and why, how to effectively use reverse psychology, and why we get lazier when we're surrounded by more people. These were things I could immediately see and feel in my daily life.

But the biggest takeaway from my degree was that so many of our decisions are made subconsciously and without any awareness on our part. There might be clear reasons to act logically in a given circumstance—and we just might ignore all of them for no apparent reason. Our conscious thought follows our subconscious will, and it often isn't until far after we act that we figure out what actually happened.

For example, one of the more famous experiments in psychology was called the Little Albert experiment. It involved a baby, Little Albert, who was presented with a white rat and nothing else. He had no reaction, positive or negative. Albert had yet to be conditioned or socialized in any way regarding rats.

Next, the researchers paired the rat with a loud crashing noise, which frightened Albert and made him cry in most instances. After only a couple of exposures with the rat and the crashing noise, Albert was presented with the rat alone again. He reacted as if the crashing noise was also present; he had become afraid of the rat by itself.

He had started associating the rat with the loud noise that frightened him and wasn't consciously aware of why he was suddenly recoiling and crying whenever he saw the rat by itself. It was a fascinating discovery about how something seemingly so subtle and unrelated could affect people's actions in very real ways.

If people can be subconsciously conditioned about negative associations, aren't there ways that people can be conditioned to react positively to objects and people? What if Little Albert was conditioned to associate positive things with the rat, such as food or his favorite toy? This would make Albert rejoice upon seeing the rat instead of recoiling in horror.

This brings us to the most famous psychological experiment of the modern age: Ivan Pavlov's dog.

Pavlov, a Russian psychologist, noted that his dog began to salivate when he anticipated a meal. Pavlov began to ring a bell every time he fed his dog and paired the two behaviors together: the bell and the dog salivating. When Pavlov started simply ringing the bell by itself, the dog salivated as if there was actual food coming. Without any real clue as to why, the dog thought he was getting bacon every time he heard the bell.

Little Albert and Pavlov's dog showed us two sides of the same coin—it is possible for us to become scientifically and subconsciously desired. If a bell can create a positive effect on others, there must be additional, more impactful ways of being scientifically likable. My mission with this book is to uncover the most effective, peer-reviewed psychological studies to dig deep and take advantage of what human nature can offer us.

These studies run the gamut from confirmatory to shocking and counterintuitive, but that's because we are still figuring out how our brains truly work. You'll learn proven ways to make yourself endearing, likable, funny, convincing, persuasive, trustworthy, credible, and instantly magnetic. You'll learn why we hit it off with some people but never with others; why we feel chemistry with some people and instantly mutter, "Ugh, not them," in the presence of others; and why we instinctively trust some people and check for our wallets around others.

Some you might not believe if there wasn't evidence, and some might even feel commonsensical—but that's because you understand it on a deeper, subconscious, and instinctual level. All of that and more is *The Science of Likability*. Our CEOs, politicians, and most charismatic friends are all doing *something* right. Now it's your turn.

Chapter 1. How to Improve People's Moods

Why do some people instantly like us while others seem to instantly hold a grudge?

Is hitting it off and becoming friends with people purely a roll of the dice? Or is there something more we can do to control our chances of connecting with people? If it's just chance, then why do some people seem to be able to connect with anyone while others appear to be virtually invisible?

For many people, likability seems to be a game of chance. If you happen to sit next to someone who is similar to you, and you also happen to have an excuse to begin a conversation with them, only then are you on the highway to friendship. Statistically, that can't happen with every new friend we make, so that doesn't sound quite right.

People who see likability as completely organic and natural are sadly misguided, because cultivating a feeling of likability around yourself is just like any other emotion—it can be triggered, summoned, eliminated, and ultimately engineered. If we want to make someone angry with us, we know what to do and how to adjust our behavior. If we want to make someone cry, we also know how to create that feeling. Likability is not much different; it's only a far more desirable outcome.

It turns out that we all have specific and subtle signals and hints that massively influence the way we view others and how they view us. Most of them are miniscule, subconscious, and mired in the minutiae—but these are the details that actually make the difference. If you went into a restaurant and saw only one cockroach hiding in the corner, well, it might be miniscule but still quite important. These are the things you can control to stop leaving your first impression to random chance.

The first study of the book asks the following question: how can you influence and improve people's moods to make a better impression?

A 1994 study by Eich, Macauley, and Ryan found that memories did not exist in a vacuum. Memories were heavily linked to the context, environment, events, and moods that were present at the time of the memory. This means memory is not a flat representation of a set of events—it's a holistic, three-dimensional snapshot of everything that was happening at that exact moment in time. Whatever else you were experiencing at the time is linked to the memory and can be used to bring it back up.

We don't realize this because much of what is recorded in our memory banks is subconsciously etched. But it's in there *somewhere*, and Eich and his associates found that appealing to those hidden aspects of memories allows you to influence people's moods for the better.

In this study, the researchers created situations to put the participants in either good or bad moods. Then the subjects were given neutral words and asked what type of memories the neutral words evoked. Participants who were in good moods typically recalled positive memories, while participants who were in bad moods typically recalled negative memories. This finding exemplified a simple truth: memory and mood are inexorably linked, and manipulating one can manipulate the other.

In other words, if we think about happy memories, our mood rises, and if we think about dreadful memories, our mood plummets. By itself, it's not a huge revelation. If you think about puppies and kittens, you are likely to smile and laugh and get cheered up. But never before had it been shown that our moods can be so intimately tied to the memories that we think about at that moment in time. By understanding this process, we can do this to ourselves and to others.

That's how you can become a preternatural force at improving the moods of the people around you. If you are able to accurately invoke elements that were present at the time of a positive memory (recall how holistic and three-dimensional memory is), people will unconsciously slip into the mood they were in during that memory.

For instance, suppose you know your friend Dorothy's best moment in life was when she got married. Her wedding was in a garden with lots of balloons, pillows, and flowers. She had a themed wedding where everyone wore black and silver as a tribute to her favorite band, KISS. Presumably she was in a good mood that day.

So what would you do to improve Dorothy's mood?

You would indirectly display or reference things that would remind her of that day. You might play KISS music in the background, you might talk to her outside in a garden, and you might wear a black and silver shirt. You might even bring up a wedding you were at recently, since she has such a fond memory of weddings. Ask about her wedding directly. Maybe none of these things in isolation would impact Dorothy's mood, but taken together, these are powerful, indirect reminders and cues for one of her best memories. She will pick up on that, and her mood will perk up—though she may not understand why.

What does this mean for us?

People's moods and memory are highly linked. If you get a clear idea that someone is in need of a mood boost, you can talk about things, people, and events that were present when they were in fabulous moods. Reference their greatest triumphs or fondest memories.

Talk to people in terms of what makes them happy. It's not a radical notion, but it's not one we are taught to consider. When we want to improve people's moods, our first inclination might be to simply make a joke or utilize a distraction like two entire pizzas. Those approaches are attempting to indirectly deal with mood while referencing memories is a direct way to change it.

Take advantage of your knowledge of someone and pull them out of the doldrums by triggering their great memories.

To make this dynamic work most effectively for you, you must first accurately determine people's moods. We're not always able to tell if someone is truly happy or sad because people are often socialized to not wear their hearts on their sleeves. This is doubly true in corporate or office environments where the exposure of someone's true mental state can be seen as unprofessional.

Eich and the other researchers devised a method to determine people's mood simply by asking them a neutral question. The underlying assumption they relied upon was that people will react to a neutral question in a way that reflects how they feel. The answer isn't important; it's about whether people answer in a non-neutral way.

The easiest question to ask is simply, "How is your day?" or "How is your week going?" It will usually be easy to tell how people are feeling based on their body language and tone of voice in answering these questions. If someone answers you in a lukewarm tone, seems anxious about something, or outright talks about how annoying someone or something is, you're in a prime position to improve their mood.

Then, as the study showed, bring up elements that were present in one of their positive memories. If you know James had a blast the last time he went skiing, bring up a story he's told about it. Have him retell it to you. Ask him about the logistics and whether or not he would recommend that particular ski lodge. Talk about the games he played that weekend. Casually reference a video of skiing tricks. Likewise, if James loved biking: you could mention their greatest biking adventure, their longest ride, their favorite bike, their biking buddies, or their latest gear purchase.

By bringing up the memory elements that were tied to the happy mood they were probably in at the time, you will improve their current mood. It makes sense that people like to discuss their favorite topics, but now there is a deeper psychological understanding of why and what it does to someone. Like Pavlov's dog, this isn't a process that we are fully aware of until we reach the end result of suddenly salivating.

Eich's study was about influencing people's moods, not necessarily improving them. In the context of likability, the only way you should be influencing people's moods is positively, but this subconscious superpower can be used to take people's moods in any direction you wish. It just won't necessarily give you a pleasant outcome and subsequent association. No one is drawn to the person that reminds them of the last funeral they went to.

There is another benefit of improving someone's mood: the power of association.

If you play your cards right, people will subconsciously start associating their happy moods with *you*. When you are successful in creating a happy mood or dragging someone out from the dumps consistently, they can't help but feel drawn to you, and they will begin to associate you with those positive feelings. You become part of their pleasant memory, and they begin to be drawn to you without a conscious understanding of why.

As you'll discover, one of the running themes of this book is that human beings may seem very complex and nuanced, but often we make choices that are very straightforward and predictable—for instance, avoiding pain and seeking pleasure. You can come up with many theories about the motivations people have for certain things, but it's a very simple subconscious process the vast majority of the time.

We tend to gravitate toward people who make us feel good and away from things that hurt us. We also gravitate toward people and things *associated* with the people who make us feel good, and this is called classical conditioning. Remember Pavlov's dog? He would salivate in the presence of positive reinforcement and eventually was conditioned to salivate to only the sound of a bell. When people subconsciously begin to associate you with positive moods and emotions, you are going to be the bell that makes people smile without realizing why.

Byrne and Clore in 1970 expanded on Pavlov's findings and discovered that if people are nearby when we feel good, even if they were not involved in creating the positive feelings, eventually we begin to feel good whenever they are around. In other words, you can become the bell and your presence alone can inspire positive feelings.

Creating or being present during people's great moods is one way to become associated with their happiness and for them to want you around. It's like if you're a baker and you need a rare kind of flour for your favorite cake. If you see the rare flour, you know you are going to have a chance to bake your favorite cake. It's not about the flour, and it's not about you. It's what you represent and are associated with.

There are two other main ways through which we can take advantage of being liked because others associate us with great feelings.

First, positivity pays off. People enjoy being happy, so they will naturally want to be around the causes of their happiness. They would rather not be dragged into other people's problems and have to listen to other people's personal tragedies.

You'd be surprised how effective staying in a good mood, putting on a happy face, praising others, and complimenting others can be. In our modern world, there are a lot of unpleasant people, and most people are too absorbed in their own muck to be cheerful to others. If you are that one ray of sunshine in an otherwise dreary day, you will be a memorable anomaly.

People will associate positive feelings with you and subconsciously want to spend time around you—it's the brain's way of telling them to continue letting them produce endorphins. In fact, one easy way is to bring food to any gathering you attend. People will begin to welcome your presence regardless of the occasion, and they won't even realize that it may be because of the food instead of your shining personality. They'll just want you around, period.

I want to reiterate and emphasize how important compliments can be. Most people don't receive compliments on a daily basis. By giving someone even a shallow or cursory compliment, you might be 100% of their compliments for the entire day. This isn't something that will go unnoticed. Compliment them on something shallow, their personality, or their opinion. Pay attention especially to compliments you can pay in recognizing something that someone has put effort into. Just put someone in a position to say thank-you. This shows an extra layer of thought and care.

Finally, you can flat-out associate yourself with people's favorite things. If someone loves skiing, you can do any of the following:

- Talk about skiing
- Ask about skiing
- Show them pictures of skiing
- Ski with them
- Compare notes on skiing

If people enjoy something and they start to think of you when they think about their favorite hobby, it's almost too easy. In other words, if someone loves ice cream, bring ice cream to a gathering or go with them to their favorite ice cream parlor. Do a little bit of research, and then present yourself with what they love.

Improving people's moods is about more than the mood itself. It's about how you become magnetic and likable overall. You represent positive feelings in such a way that it's not even about you as a person or how well you click with someone. People can consciously like you and your personality, but slipping into someone's good graces subconsciously is just as powerful.

Takeaways:

- Most people tend to rely on luck or happenstance to strike up friendships and be likable. This is the wrong approach because it undermines your own abilities. One of the ways we can make friends more easily and have better impressions is by improving people's moods.
- Improving people's moods involves invoking times they were already in a good mood from their memory banks, because memory is heavily context-dependent. As an added bonus, once you are able to create a good mood in others, you yourself become part of those memories, and they are positively conditioned to enjoy your presence.
- Other ways to improve people's moods

include positivity, generating goodwill, and associating yourself with things people like and enjoy. Compliments are another easy way to do this on a daily basis.

Chapter 2. How to Turn Enemies into Friends

Most people in our lives fall into the vast gray area between friend and enemy.

That's because most of the people we know are actually neutral acquaintances. You wouldn't invite them to your wedding, and you wouldn't cry if they got fired from their job. You might miss them occasionally if you were to move or change occupations, but you don't try to make plans with them on the weekend. In many cases, you could take them or leave them. They're friends of convenience—pretty much the people who inhabit your high school reunions. It's nice to see them, but if they're not in front of you,

you might not remember that they exist. It's unrealistic to have a high degree of investment in so many people.

The enemies, however, we never seem to be rid of. Some people's faces just annoy us or send us into fits of rage—and your face likely does the same for a select few. Maybe you unknowingly cut someone off in traffic and made a new enemy there. It happens, and such is life. No one is everyone's cup of tea, and that's okay. Cats are destined to hate dogs most of the time; some temperaments or personalities are fated to never mix and match.

The big difference between an enemy (or *frenemy*, as it were) and a real friend is the intent from which they act. A friend might do harsh things with the intent to help you and improve your life—they always mean well. It's where the phrase *tough love* comes from.

An enemy, on the other hand, always means to do you harm. Even if they do arguably positive things for you, their real underlying motivation is to harm you in some way. They might actually do a good thing for you and help you out, but at the end of the day, they actually want you to slip up. They're not looking out for your best interests, especially if those interests conflict with theirs.

Even if you don't think you have any true enemies, and just a couple of people you prefer to mock and make fun of, it would still be nice to be able to convert them into something resembling friends. You never know when you might need them, after all. The science of likability can help you win people over just as well as it can help you make a splash of an impression.

According to studies, it Is actually easier to turn an enemy into a friend than you realize, and they may not even realize that it's happening. They'll just notice they have fewer and fewer negative feelings toward you and less of a compulsion to curse your name. Sometimes that's as good as anything.

This was a phenomenon first observed by

Benjamin Franklin, one of the founding fathers of the United States of America, and later proved and confirmed by Jecker and Landy in 1969. The latter pair were investigating Benjamin Franklin's claim that he could easily turn an enemy into a friend with one simple act—asking *them* for a favor.

That's right—*asking* that person for a favor instead of *performing* a favor for that person. This seems counterintuitive and confusing, because first of all, why would someone want to do anything for someone they dislike? Second of all, wouldn't this make the other person resent you for daring to ask a favor when you are not liked by them?

Usually, you would only do a favor for somebody if you already liked them and wanted them to like you. You would want to impress them and make your value known. You'd be willing to make the effort because you care about them.

Therefore, you'd think people would balk at doing something for someone they hate.

That's what conventional knowledge would say. However, Jecker and Landy confirmed that participants liked a researcher who'd asked them for a small favor far more than they liked the researcher who hadn't asked for one. They split the participants into three groups:

- The first group was asked to return the reward for participating in the study because the researcher had run low on funds.
- The second group was asked to return the money because the research department had run low on funds.
- The third group was not asked anything and was allowed to keep the money.

Which group favored its researcher most? The first group, followed by the third group, liked its researcher the most. A direct favor that actually took money out of their pockets made participants like their researcher more than the group who got to keep their money. As odd as this seems, it confirms the fact that making someone act for you, at their detriment, can make them like you more. So why does the Benjamin Franklin effect work?

When you ask someone to do you a favor, you force people to justify their actions to themselves. "Wait, I just did this for Johnson. Why would I do something like that? What does this say about me and how I feel about him?"

In a twist, they will tell themselves this and actually start liking you more because they, deep down inside, feel some type of affection, respect, or interest in their enemies. This is the concept of *cognitive dissonance*, which Leon Festinger developed in the 1960s. Cognitive dissonance is essentially the resolution of a conflict between people's views, thoughts, and actions.

For instance, if we believe we dislike someone and then we take the action of doing something for them, cognitive dissonance dictates that there is conflict and tension in the person's mind. These are two beliefs that are in direct opposition: "I hate them" and "I did a favor for them." Thus, to alleviate the tension, a clever explanation will pop up and make the opposing stances reconcilable. With the Benjamin Franklin effect, why would you do something for your archenemy? Because you actually like them and want to help them. It's your brain's clever attempt to make sense of the world and your conflicting beliefs.

Asking someone to perform a favor for you is also a subtle form of flattery. Imagine you are asking your nemesis at the office to help you with a report. The implication isn't that you're lazy or stupid. Rather, the implication is a greater recognition of their prowess as a whole. In other words, you recognize they are so skilled at what they do that you are willing to risk embarrassment to ask them for their help. You are submitting, showing your belly, and admitting to them you would like their help.

Finally, asking someone for a favor is just more interaction between you two, whereas there was previously zero. You likely avoid people you don't like or brush them off. You start to develop stereotypes about them, and the more psychological distance, the more apathy grows. This isn't helping matters. When you ask for a favor, you are probably doing it in a kind way and humanizing yourself to others. The more information they have about you, the less they are likely to hate the version of you they've constructed in their heads.

It can still be a thought contrary to common sense, so what does the Benjamin Franklin effect mean for us?

Asking people to do you a small favor will make you more likable, regardless of if they like you or hate you. It can't be too big, otherwise you will burden them and give the impression that you are lazy or entitled. It can't be too small, otherwise people will think you are lazy or entitled. People will react the same if you skew too far to either side of the spectrum: asking someone to write your report versus asking someone to hold the door for you will garner the same ire either way.

If you can't think of an appropriate favor to ask of your enemies or frenemies, a helpful guideline is the three-minute rule. Ask them for something that will take no longer or shorter than three minutes. Don't burden them unnecessarily, but don't make it seem like you are hopeless and helpless.

Each of these subtle favors will cause a state of massive cognitive dissonance, wherein your enemies will try to make sense of contradicting themselves. The winner out of that mental confusion is you, because they inevitably rationalize that you're not so bad, after all.

Beyond the Benjamin Franklin effect, you can also perform small, subtle favors for your enemies and frenemies. Now this is something intuitive and easily understood. Actively performing favors for others builds goodwill and indicates a willingness to be friendly and open. You are raising the white flag of peace and sending the signal that you don't harbor any ill will.

At the very least, if you perform small favors, your enemies won't classify you as completely useless but as someone with *some* value. At best, doing favors will neutralize whatever initial animosity they may have had for you. And on your side, as the Benjamin Franklin effect dictates, you will feel more positively about the people you perform favors for. It works on yourself as well.

You are giving enemies an opportunity to view you in a more nuanced or complex light. This is quite a step forward, because people often stereotype each other along very simplistic lines: *friend good, enemy bad*.

When you throw your enemies a curveball by being kind to them, you blur the lines and they can't help but come up with a different way of viewing you. There's a reason that "kill them with kindness" is often parroted!

If you receive questions from your enemies about your motives and why you're suddenly so nice to them, talk about how you do favors for everyone in general—this part is important, or else they might feel that you are trying to manipulate them.

Don't expect any payback or reciprocation—this will help reduce their concern over manipulation or ulterior motives. Plus, only acting if you receive something in return is a toxic mindset you should shake. Focus instead on the fact that you are acting to change how somebody feels about you. People can be quite vicious, but they're also easily disarmed.

The next time you ask that same favor, you may be surprised at how positive the reaction is. *And* you get a favor performed for you? Win-win. You can generate enough goodwill to reach across the aisle with this surprising tip for likability. Your enemies may not be aware of what's happening, and that's the best part.

Takeaways:

- You might be the friendliest and most

benign person in the world, and still you will offend someone. That's just the reality of life, but you don't have to take it lying down.

- An easy way to turn an enemy into a friend is with the Benjamin Franklin effect, where you invoke cognitive dissonance by asking an enemy to perform a small favor for you. They will justify to themselves that you are not so bad after all if they performed a favor for you. In addition, you are initiating contact, which tends to humanize others.

- A final way to turn an enemy into a friend is to perform favors for them. This is more intuitive and easily understood—if you present value to someone, they will like you more. Or at least, they won't consider you completely useless, and that's the best we can do with some people. The goal is to blur the lines people have created in their minds and make it easier to be accepted.

Chapter 3. How to Create the Foundation of Friendship

It's rude to look at your friendships and evaluate them based on how much you are benefiting from them. In essence, are your friendships and relationships purely transactional? Nobody likes to think this way—at least, not out loud.

We would love to imagine that we are friends with our friends because they suit us the best, we enjoy their company, and they know us inside and out. We all inhabit a special place in each other's hearts because of our unique sensibilities and emotional bonds, right? It sounds nice to say, and it's the politically correct version of how to describe friendships, new and old.

But in reality, people subconsciously evaluate their relationships based on how much value they get from such relationships. It's important to mention that value is subjective and doesn't necessarily have to be in the form of any material or financial gain. Of course, we do value people who are valuable connections based on their wealth or status, but we also value people if they make us laugh, make us feel good, or act as our emotional crutches.

Value in a friendship or relationship is usually measured in *emotional terms*. If people make us feel positive emotions, they have value to us, and we want them around because of their emotional value proposition. If they make us feel negative emotions, then we might not want them around, no matter how much they would be able to help our careers.

It's fair to say relationships are inherently a bit transactional. We get what we want from people in some form or fashion, and our friends get what they want from us in similar fashion. If you spend time with someone who's company you don't enjoy, but these events always occur on their private yacht, it might be acceptable because you're hanging out on a yacht. But remove the yacht, and what are you getting in this transaction?

Here's the thing about transactions: they only feel good if they are relatively equal. One-sided deals or relationships feel bad. We're happiest when the give and take, or cost and benefit, are roughly equal. You wouldn't sell someone your car for $2 because it would be spectacularly one-sided and you'd feel ripped off. You also wouldn't buy someone's car for $2 because you'd feel guilty and immoral. However, you would sell someone your car for a fair price or trade them for the motorcycle you've always wanted.

If a transaction is one-sided, we feel used and taken advantage of or predatory and vicious. If you always give someone a ride to work and they never return the favor or acknowledge your effort, you aren't going to feel good about the relationship anymore because the transaction is unbalanced.

It seems cold to categorize relationships thusly, but it is something that has been proven to be running in the background at all times. It's not unhealthy to think about your relationships in terms of transactions, as long as you can maintain some flexibility. Would you want to be in an unbalanced friendship where someone used you for financial or emotional support yet always turned their back to you when you needed it?

A study showed that people are likely to subconsciously or consciously keep track of the exchange of favors in their relationships— and those are the happiest relationships. You can use this knowledge to your advantage in becoming a more likable person, as well as one who never gets taken advantage of.

Walster, Walster, and Berscheid proposed the *theory of equal relationships* in 1978. They investigated how relationships rife with inequity functioned and found that the best and happiest relationships have an internal score sheet as to who is sacrificing and serving more. In these relationships, both sides sought to keep it equal. As mentioned, people won't want to feel like predators *or* prey.

This can range from monetary ("I'll pay for tonight if you pay for tomorrow") to emotional tradeoffs. They found people are often driven by a sense of equality, which means that they will overcompensate if they feel they are not holding up their end of the bargain, so to speak. More broadly, the study helped further articulate what is known as equity theory—the tendency for humans to compare what they have in relation to others (Adams, 1963).

Equity theory holds that people seek to get as much as they can in any given relationship. And yet, if someone gets too much or too little, even according to the set rules of engagement, tension and distress are created in the person's mind. The greater the inequality in a relationship, the greater tension and distress.

We are constantly at war between these two conflicting desires: for the most possible and for relative equality. Therefore, one of the foundations of friendship is a feeling of equality.

Suppose we are sitting at a table with one friend and there is a small pizza on the table. We both love pizza, so we both want as much as possible. Yet we also know that the pizza should be split in half to acknowledge the other person and show goodwill in the friendship. But it's our favorite type of pizza, and we want all of it and could easily eat it.

What would happen if you accidentally took an extra slice? You would feel guilty and your friend would probably show restrained annoyance and anger.

What about if you took an extra slice on purpose? You would probably feel like a heel, and your friend would be supremely unhappy.

This is the case even if our friend were to tell us, "I love this pizza, but take as much as you want." We wouldn't want to upset the balance, and most people would still split the pizza in half. Anything else just feels greedy and inconsiderate.

What does equity theory mean for us? Should we seek to pull out a score card and annotate every time a debt is incurred?

Surprisingly, yes. At least, mentally. Keeping score as to the equality of your relationships will make you more likable. When you externally acknowledge equity theory and make it known you are fighting your human tendency to take as much as possible, people will take notice. If you can keep yourself accountable and actively seek to even the score, you become more likable.

It doesn't necessarily have to be so direct as, "You bought me coffee last time, so I will buy it today." Remember, the transactional nature of a relationship doesn't solely concern finances or material possessions—it is subjective. To keep the score even, you should also consider emotional support: listening, time, attention, focus, and any and all other aspects that you value. If someone listens to you for an hour, remember that, in some nebulous way, you owe them a degree of emotional support at another time.

Underlying everything is the fact that people hate feeling guilty (when they *take* too much) and also hate feeling taken advantage of (when they *give* too much). If there is inequality in any measure, both parties will feel one of those emotions.

If someone continually fixes a friend's car, they might start to feel resentment and injustice. They'll feel like they are being taken advantage of and won't see the value of that friendship. The friend who owns that car, on the other hand, will feel burdened by debt, guilt, and insecurity in the friendship.

People do not like to be in somebody else's debt. People do not like to feel that their friend is giving them more than they give their friend. Loudly seeking equity in friendships and creating equal status avoids issues like that. Our egalitarian natures lead us to expecting others to hold up their end of the bargain. In other words, since you and I are equal, we expect each other to be self-reliant, responsible, and self-sufficient. I can't view you as an equal if you're constantly depending on me. The mere acknowledgment of that fact can show the self-awareness necessary to dispel most of these negative thoughts.

Use the feeling of equity to your advantage and make sure that you make it known that you are on equal footing with your friend. Eliminate the other person's feelings of guilt (when they take too much) and injustice (when they give too much).

If you see any situations where you benefit more, call them out publicly and make sure to rectify them as soon as possible. This makes the other person know that you pay your debts as soon as possible and are trustworthy and that you actively care about them and don't want to cheat them. Of course, this also removes the burden of feeling taken advantage of from their head.

For example, you can eliminate some resentment and injustice when you call out, "I can't believe that you gave me a ride to the airport and I haven't repaid you yet! Dinner's on me." Eliminating guilt on the other person's behalf is trickier because it's difficult to say something like, "Hey, I got you last time we had dinner. Want to even that score?" You must tread carefully, because this can sound offensive and entitled.

Even if it doesn't quite make things equal, it just lets the other person know your honest, self-aware character. Oftentimes, you won't have to do anything at all except call out the inequality and show your empathy.

If you feel that you are suffering an injustice, it's simply a matter of giving people a chance to set things right. If they don't seize the opportunity, they might not be the type of person you want to remain friends with.

People are looking for win-win relationships, and you are proactively creating them. They can't help but feel that you are somebody who will stand up for your rights and that you are not a pushover or someone easily taken advantage of. That's pretty likable, right?

Equality and equity is one of the first foundations of friendship. The second foundation of friendship is similarity.

To many, bonding with others is a process that occurs over time or as a function of the passage of time. This is not always the case. You can be in a dentist's chair and undergoing a root canal, thereby spending a good amount of "alone time" with your dentist, but this is far from bonding. Something that allows you to make a bond immediately is the discovery of similarity.

This is something we instinctually do already. What are among the first questions we might ask strangers?

- Where are you from?

- Where do you live?
- Where do you work?
- Where did you go to school?

We've all experienced the phenomenon where we ask someone where they went to school and then discover they went to school where three of your acquaintances went. The next question out of our mouths will inevitably be some version of, "Oh, my friends went there. Jane Smith, Bob Dinn, and John Doe. Do you know them?" The question may disregard the fact that it was a giant school and they weren't the same age, year, or major.

Why do we do this? Because we are instinctually seeking out similarities and common ground. We want to find a connection and point of reference from which to evaluate other people as quickly as possible so we know whom we are talking to. We make judgments on people very quickly, and if they are similar to us, our judgments will tend to be more positive.

In 1971, Donn Byrne studied what we all instinctually already knew. He found that we are more drawn and attracted to people who show greater degrees of similarity to us. The relationship was found to be nearly linear—the more similarity, the more affection or attraction. He conducted a simple experiment that asked participants to fill out a questionnaire on their personal traits. The participants were shown fake profiles of people that had been manipulated to be similar or dissimilar to them, and the more similar the traits of the profiles, the more attractive the participants marked them.

We like similarity, and not just because we tend to have a positive opinion of ourselves. We like similarity in all respects because of the positive assumptions we can make about them. We like ourselves, after all, so we should naturally like people similar to us.

For instance, let's say you were born in a small town in South America. Now you live in London. How excited would you be at the prospect of meeting someone else from that same small South American town?

Now, what additional assumptions would you make about them?

- You share the same values.
- You have a similar worldview.
- They automatically "get you" in a way that others may not.
- You are similar in personality.
- You can make inside jokes that no one else will understand.
- You generally know them as a person.

All of these assumptions are positive. They might even be true in most instances. You suddenly have a point of reference through which to view your new friend, which is comforting. You aren't working with a blank slate anymore, and you generally will know this person's thought process.

If you discovered you share a similarity of enjoying the same sport, you can make many assumptions about the person and immediately start using that sport's lingo. The more obscure, rare, or unique the similarity, the more we like the person who shares that with us, because the more special it becomes.

We like people who are similar to us in background, attitude, and opinions. Just like in a previous chapter, you can't wait for the possibility to present itself, such as randomly seeing the mascot of a university at a restaurant and then realizing you went to the same college. This means we should always be *searching* for similarities or *creating* them. They both take effort and initiative.

We can *search* for similarities by asking probing questions of people and using their answers as the basis to show similarity, no matter how small. Ask questions to figure out what people are about, what they like, and how they think. Then dig deep into yourself to find small commonalities at first, such as favorite baseball teams or alcoholic drinks. Through those smaller commonalities, you'll be able to figure out what makes them tick and find deeper commonalities to instantly bond over. Just as you'd be thrilled to meet someone from that small South American town, you'd be thrilled to meet someone who shared a love of the same obscure hobby as you.

It doesn't take months or years, and it doesn't take a special circumstance like going through boot camp together. It just requires you to look outside of yourself and realize that people share common attitudes, experiences, and emotions—you just have to find them. Get comfortable asking questions and digging deeper than you naturally would. (Is it odd for you to ask five questions in a row? It shouldn't be.) It might even feel a little invasive at first. Find them and use them!

We can *create* similarities by mimicking people's body language, voice tonality, rate of speech, and overall manner of appearance. This is known as *mirroring*, and it has also been shown to produce feelings of positivity when tested (Anderson, 1998). All you have to do is arrange yourself to resemble others in order to benefit from feelings of similarity, from how they are posed to how they gesture.

If you were a caveman, you would only seek out similar people because anything else presented a threat to your life, from different tribes to feline hunters. We're not cavemen anymore, but similarity and familiarity are still comforting and allow us to let out a deep breath of relief. Sometimes it can be conscious, but mostly it is a subconscious tactic you can use to have people quickly relax and open up around you.

If you can cultivate feelings of similarity and combine them with an air of equity in your friendships right off the bat, the foundations for friendship will have been laid. After all, no one dislikes the person who reminds them of themselves *and* insists on paying you back or treating you to dinner. Sometimes common sense *is* common.

Takeaways:

- Equity and feelings of fairness play a large part in the foundation of friendship. That is to say, people don't like the negative feelings associated with either side of unfairness. They don't like feeling like they are being used, nor do they like feeling like they are cheating someone. Therefore, emphasize fair play and equity in terms of the value (which is subjective and can vary widely) you are putting into a relationship or friendship.

- Similarity is another large aspect of the foundation of friendship. We like those who are similar to ourselves instinctively. These days, we take similarity to mean a higher chance of bonding and matching worldviews and positive traits.

- Humans are more similar to each other than not. We all bleed and put our pants on one leg at a time. Therefore, it is up to you to either search for or create similarities. You can *search* for similarities by becoming comfortable with questions and the feeling that you are being slightly invasive, and you can *create* similarities using the psychological phenomenon of mirroring.

Chapter 4. How to Act the Part

If you've never been to an intense sporting event, allow me to describe the general atmosphere.

In a word, it's mayhem. The entire crowd is there for a purpose: to cheer on one of the teams. It is tribalism to the extreme. People have taken the effort to drag themselves out to the sporting event, pay exorbitant prices for food and drink, and sit in uncomfortable and crowded chairs. None of that matters; it is a small sacrifice for the excitement and fervor they have for one of the teams playing.

People will scream at the top of their lungs

and engage in a cheering frenzy anytime something positive happens for their team. This drive for victory can turn some people into hooligans, and in recent years, there have even been fans killed by other fans for being on the wrong side. And you know what? You're going to get sucked right into it. Perhaps not to that extent, but it's highly contagious, and you will become a product of your environment. You will cheer and scream, even if it's not in your nature. This is your new normal, as long as you are in that environment.

This everyday example demonstrates how often we take cues from others on how to act. We see what it takes to blend in and act the part in any context we find ourselves in. This is also how we can become more likable—by seeing how close friends act and *acting the part of a close friend.*

If you treat someone like a stranger or acquaintance, that's how they will treat you back. If you keep someone at arm's length, very rarely will they make the effort to break down your barriers. Thus, by acting the part of a familiar friend, you become more likable. According to Sigmund Freud's *theory of transference*, acting similarly to someone else will make people treat you like that person. It brings up feelings of familiarity, and you naturally fall into that relationship dynamic of the person you are acting similarly to. Therefore, act like a good friend, and people will see and welcome you like one.

Freud is famous for many theories.

First, of course, there is his theory on the Oedipus complex, which states that we are forever in subconscious sexual competition with our same-sex parent because we want to have sex with our opposite-sex parent. In other words, sons want to have sex with their mothers, and daughters want to have sex with their fathers and supplant the other parent at the head of the family. This theory doesn't typically hold much weight with modern psychologists, though there are frequent armchair observations such as dating people that are similar to your opposite-sex parent.

Second, Freud proposed that the greatest source of tension and discomfort within people was the everlasting battle between the *ego, id*, and *superego*. The id is the part of the psyche that is primal and only seeks to satisfy basic human drives such as sex, food, and shelter. The id is mostly hidden from others and suppressed because it is not considered appropriate or acceptable.

The superego can be said to be opposite of the id because it seeks to conform to rules of society and utilize a sense of right and wrong. The ego is said to regulate both drives and make them able to work together and be expressed in a healthy manner. It moderates between our desires and what is acceptable behavior-wise. This is still up for debate and popular in modern discourse.

Third, Freud was the first psychologist to put forth the idea that nearly all of our actions and thoughts are driven by subconscious desire, to some degree. Sometimes subconscious desires leak out through dreams or slips of the tongue (known as Freudian slips).

He was a busy man. His theory that most contributes to the science of likability is transference—the idea that if you act the part, people will begin to *transfer* feelings they have about other people onto you. If you act the part of a close friend, people will begin to transfer the feelings they have about their close friends to you.

For instance, many people with strong supervisors feel paternal or maternal transference because of the similar roles those authority figures play in their lives. Others may feel close to counselors or coaches because of how much personal information they reveal to them. This transference of feelings occurs because people feel that they are interacting with a parent or close friend, respectively. Generating this feeling of intimacy is how transference can benefit you.

You can act the part in many ways. You can embody specific characteristics of their close friends. You can act familiar and like you've known them for years. You can take on a role similar to that of someone they are close to. You can treat them in the same way their close friend does. The overall message of transference is to find a pattern of behavior that appeals to the person and emulate it.

Human beings navigate the world through snapshots that we know, and we try to apply those snapshots to unfamiliar situations. We have general snapshots of people as well— good and bad. Within these snapshots, feelings, habits, emotions, and mannerisms are included. This is useful for making quick decisions and deciding if we like someone or if we feel threatened by them.

Human beings might be imaginative, but we are also very lazy and efficient to a fault, so we try to put all our experiences into existing templates and snapshots based on our previous experiences.

If you consciously try to fit into the snapshot of a good friend and start looking and acting like one, people will better understand how to treat you and interact with you. Fit the snapshot of a good friend who lends emotional support and you will position yourself well. The beauty of transference is that this happens subconsciously and people aren't aware they are making this association. If you simply act like a close friend, you'll trigger the association.

On a more general note, do away with pleasantries and formalities and get into the habit of speaking to people the way you speak to your best friends. Talk about intimate matters. Joke with them and act familiar. Be there for them emotionally and support them through whatever they are going through. Skip the small talk questions about their job or upbringing.

Show none of the hesitancy or unfamiliarity that strangers have with each other. Don't be afraid to touch them and create inside jokes immediately. That's how friends act, and it's not until you articulate the difference that you realize you are preventing people from getting close to you by treating them like strangers. You might be surprised to find that you are setting the very tone you are unhappy with.

Never think, "Is it okay that I ask about this?" or "Am I going too far?" That's not what close friends do. You'll be surprised at how people will open up and the subsequent effect on how they receive you.

This might mean you are acting outside your comfort zone from time to time, but that's why you're reading this book in the first place. If it was so easy, everyone would be doing it, and you are seeking a way to improve your behaviors to achieve the outcome you want. *Fake it till you make it*, as they say. Ideally, we should be true to ourselves and "keep it real" at all times. Unfortunately, we live in an imperfect world. Oftentimes, you have to compromise to achieve practical results.

In this case, all you are doing is faking like you

are friends. That's not manipulation or misrepresentation. You're just skipping past small talk and diving into the interesting parts of people's lives. It's as simple as skipping the questions about where they work and jumping to how much fun their barbeque was because their drunk uncle was there.

Acting the part of a good friend is helpful, but just as helpful is not judging others and putting a set of expectations on them—which makes them become who we think they are.

This is known as the Pygmalion effect, named for the mythical Greek figure who fell in love with his own sculpture. It states that if you have an image of that person's behavior and personality, that's exactly who they'll become. The implication is that however you view someone, you will treat them in a way that brings that behavior out of them. If you think someone is incredibly annoying, you will be standoffish toward them and generally act in a manner that is actually annoying in and of itself, motivating them to behave annoyingly.

If you think well of someone, you will act toward them in a manner that encourages them to be better and you will give them more chances; if you think poorly of someone, you will act toward them in a manner that will make them do worse and you won't give them the benefit of the doubt.

Most commonly, if you are apathetic toward people, you will act in a way that makes them apathetic toward you, all the while calling each other boring.

The Pygmalion effect was discovered in 1979 in a study conducted on students and teacher by Robert Feldman. Students were given IQ tests, and the teachers were not told the results. However, the teachers were told that specific students composing 20% of the class were gifted and had extremely high IQs. These students were randomly selected.

At the end of the school year, the students took another IQ test, and the 20% who were randomly selected had the largest gain in IQ— the ones the teachers thought were the smartest. What did this mean? The teachers subconsciously or consciously treated them differently and gave them preferential treatment because they had a good impression of them and their intellect. The students became who the teachers thought they were. Thus, a key to likability is to have positive perceptions of people so they can become who we think they are.

Never underestimate the power of your own expectations. You create the world you reside in through your expectations. If you were told someone was charming and fascinating, you would dig deeper into their background and discover what might be interesting about them. Conversely, if you were told that same person was a boring dud, you may not even bother engaging them. Our assumptions and expectations dictate our actions and create self-fulfilling prophecies.

In another example with children, suppose one parent decided her kids were smart, while one parent decided her kids weren't the sharpest tools in the shed. The first parent would help her child with homework, get them a tutor, and make sure they were fulfilling their potential for intelligence. The second parent would ignore her child's homework and tell them to apply themselves in other ways outside the classroom, declaring them a lost cause. There would be a huge disparity in attention and emphasis on studying, and thus the kids would turn out to fulfill their parents' expectations. They receive positive or negative feedback and the cycle grows.

We like to imagine that we are treating everyone equally, but that is essentially impossible if we think poorly of them. So how can understanding the Pygmalion effect help your likability?

Assume the best of the people you're speaking with and you will start treating them in a way that makes them like you more. Recall that people become who we expect them to be, so if we expect them to be charming and kind, we will bring that out of them. Above all else, you're going to be sending 100% positive and friendly signals to everyone—people tend to respond favorably to these.

The greater question is where our assumptions of people come from. That's a whole other book, but being aware of your assumptions is key to treating others well. Focusing on treating others well and assuming the best of them is difficult, especially because much of this is subconscious. We don't tell ourselves someone is boring so we won't engage with them much; we just approach with low expectations and don't make our usual effort. By simply assuming the best of people and affording them the benefit of the doubt, you will behave around them and talk to them in a way that makes you likable.

One of your most effective weapons in assuming the best of others is to proactively create alternate explanations for anything negative you might perceive of them. For instance, if someone has a dirty shirt, they're not dirty; they are working so hard they didn't have time to wash their shirt. If someone is annoying, they are only trying to seek attention because their parents neglect them. There is always a spin you can use to put someone in a more positive light, but the choice is yours. It's only slightly more work to come up with an explanation besides "They're just a jerk," such as "They're just misunderstood."

Acting the part and allowing others to act the part underlies likability. It's more important than you might think.

Takeaways:

- Often, we treat people like strangers when we meet them. This sounds natural, but it is actually detrimental to building rapport and being likable. Treat them like a friend and they will treat you like a friend. This is backed up by the theory of transference, which states that people transfer their emotions of someone else to those they see acting in a familiar way or role.
- We don't realize it, but we have the ability

to set the tone of our relationships, and you might be causing the very source of your unhappiness by not acting the part of a friend.

- Another aspect of treating people like a friend right off the bat is to understand how the Pygmalion effect works. People live up to the expectations we give them. If we treat them like strangers, they will remain strangers. If we expect that they are interesting, we will treat them in a way that allows them to demonstrate this. All of this requires more effort on your part, but you have the ability to set the tone, so use it.

Chapter 5. How to Persuade and Negotiate Effectively

Negotiating lies in a gray area, with most people in two camps: those who think they are expert negotiators and those who are petrified of negotiation or any interaction involving disagreement or confrontation.

For the people who think they are the next great negotiator, they are likely living in a blind spot. They constantly think they've gotten great deals, but one of the hallmarks of a terrible negotiation is if you felt no tension and perceive it as having gone smoothly. Someone just pulled one over on you. For the people who think they are terrible at negotiating, they probably avoid it and accept whatever is coming without a fight. They'd rather pay more or wait longer just to avoid awkwardness and discomfort.

Most of us reside on one side of the spectrum, but that doesn't mean any of us are actually *good* at negotiating. We end up with bad deals more often than we realize, so how can we stop that?

The secret to effective negotiation can be summed up in one sentence: each party just wants to feel like they got a good deal and a win. That's it. If the other party is happy with what they're getting, then they will be all too happy to give you what you want. Of course, it doesn't matter if they are objectively getting a win or a good deal. If you can convince them that they are, that's all that matters.

Typically, the problem with this simple approach is it's too difficult to make them feel like they got a good deal because it will come at a great cost to us. But that only occurs when you view a negotiation in terms of a single pie.

Negotiations actually have multiple pies in play at all times; you just aren't aware of the alternative ones. You have to dig and find them. If you can find the pies your opponent wants while simultaneously keeping 100% of your own pies, then that's where you truly find a negotiation that benefits both of you.

So it's up to you to find out what they actually value or to reframe your proposition to them in a way that makes them feel like they got a good deal. It's easy to fall into the trap of thinking that what is important to you is important to the other side. Oftentimes, this isn't the case. In fact, in most cases, the other side doesn't at all care what's important to you.

In this chapter, I want to cover two key techniques to get a better deal from any negotiation. These techniques involve shaping the expectations and assumptions of the party you're negotiating with to create a winning scenario, and they have been proven to work time and time again. They are called the "door in the face technique" and the "foot in the door technique." Surprisingly, they are essentially opposite techniques, but they work in predictable ways when you put them into the context of human psychology and desire.

What do negotiation tactics have to do with likability? Well, proper negotiation can be done without screaming or making ultimatums. It can even be done without tension. When you find yourself in an uncomfortable position or situation, it's important to understand how to conduct yourself in a way that isn't abrasive and doesn't burn bridges. Understanding negotiation will make tough situations go smoothly and help you handle discomfort better. Instead of freezing up or saying something you don't mean, you'll be more apt to focus on the goal and maintain your relationship.

First is the *door in the face (DITF) technique,*

which was proven and confirmed by Robert Cialdini in a 1975 study.

There are two steps. The first step is to ask for a huge and borderline unreasonable amount (of money, for example) upfront. This is something you want to shock people with and have them declare that you are insane for. The second step is to back off substantially and ask for an amount that is closer to your actual goal.

By asking for the huge amount first, you will cause someone to slam the door in your face. But then, by significantly decreasing the magnitude of your request, you will cause them to open the door and consider your second offer because you will seem like you have come back to reality. The second figure feels far more reasonable than the first figure, even if it's still relatively high.

The recipient of the request feels like they have done well in the negotiation because they have brought down the asking price substantially. It seems like a win because it's a fraction of the first figure. By comparison to the second figure, you may have reduced it 50% right off the bat, not knowing that the asker intended to actually get 50% of the price. The first ask was a foil and was meant to be rejected—and rightfully so. By starting off big and getting people upset about how unreasonable your first offer is, your second or third offers will appear very reasonable indeed. It's a win for you as well.

Compare using the DITF with starting off with your reasonable offer.

In many cases, your reasonable offer will face some resistance or might even get rejected outright. It does not get considered based on its own merits. If you start with a big, unreasonable offer, people will feel good about the amount you decrease it by.

Let's take a typical salary negotiation. The DITF technique would start with you quoting an extremely high figure. Suppose you currently make $50,000 a year and ideally want to make $65,000 a year.

You: I make $50,000 now, but I am severely underpaid. I think my salary should be nearly doubled to $90,000. I know the market.

Company: That's a bit out of reach.

You: Okay, well in that case, I think $72,000 is also reasonable. I am showing good faith by lowering my request substantially and meeting you near the middle.

Company: Thank you, that's a somewhat more reasonable sum. What about $60,000?

The first offer is rejected, allowing you plenty of wiggle room to work down to the real salary you want. It's a win-win because they feel that they got a good value out of you, and you got exactly what you wanted. Here's what would happen if you were *reasonable*:

You: I make $50,000 now, but I am severely underpaid. I think my salary should be to $60,000. I know the market.

Company: That's a bit out of reach.

You: Okay, well in that case, I think $55,000 is also reasonable. I am showing good faith by lowering my request substantially and meeting you near the middle.

Company: Thank you, that's a somewhat more reasonable sum. What about $53,000?

DITF is also something you can do outside of negotiation. Suppose you want to eat at an expensive restaurant. Your first suggestion would be a restaurant that is twice as expensive. When it is inevitably refused, the one you actually want appears like a relative discount, and there will be much less resistance to it. The contrast that you present is what will spur others to pick your choice.

The second negotiation technique is called the *foot in the door (FITD) technique*, which was proven and confirmed by Arthur Beaman in a 1983 study.

This is close to the opposite of the DITF technique. There are also two steps. First, you ask for small favors or concessions—anything to gain a degree of agreement or compliance and an open mind in the person across from you. The second step is to gradually work up to your desired ask.

The idea is that saying yes once is the most important part of a negotiation, and once you receive a yes, it's a green light that they are open for business. They've already let their guards down for you, so you must take advantage of their compliance.

This is a completely different approach than the DITF technique. Instead of starting big, you start miniscule. Of course, this is not your real offer. You are just using this tiny offer to get people to say yes to you at any scale. The key is to create a chain of yes that starts from the first figure. This is a win because at no point does the other person feel that they are making a *big* concession; a series of small concessions doesn't have quite the same impact, even if it adds up the same.

Your goal with that figure is to gain agreement and goodwill with the other person. Once they agree, you can then start to gradually add 5% here and there, based on additional points and reasons. Eventually, they will add up to something significant. Let's take the same salary negotiation from before and use the FITD technique.

You: I make $50,000 now, but I am underpaid. I think my salary should go up at least a tiny bit right now, maybe to $51,500?
Company: That seems reasonable.
You: Okay, well in that case, what about $52,500? I did hit my sales goals four months earlier than everyone else.
Company: Yes, that also seems reasonable in light of that accomplishment. How about $52,500, then?
You: Well, that would be good, but I also [insert various job performance metrics and accomplishments]. All of those things, including inflation and cost of living, add up to about $60,000. I can show you on my chart here.

You started low, got them to say yes and go along with your mode of thinking, and then gradually ratcheted up your ask with additional reasons for each additional ask. At the end, you've arrived at your goal with plenty of justification and backup. They feel that they've won because you've presented your case so well, and they feel justified in paying you that much. You deserve it, and you earned it. You obviously feel like you've won because you are getting paid what you want. Recall that if both parties are happy with the outcome in the end, that's a great negotiation.

Both of these techniques take advantage of comparison and expectation. DITF makes your goal appear reasonable by comparison, while FITD makes your goal appear reasonable and justified. Persuasion and negotiation are more than these two techniques, but they are fantastic for simply getting what you want and allowing others to feel good about it.

Becoming good at negotiation is more than getting a good deal. Oftentimes, you don't want to burn bridges or cause unnecessary tension. That's what the tactics in this chapter do—they create win-win situations where both parties feel good.

If you become good at negotiation, you also

become more likable because the people in both camps—those who think they are good and those who think they are terrible at negotiation—will either admire or respect you. Negotiation is seen as a difficult skill to master because it is inherently adversarial and conflict-driven. It takes someone who can navigate multiple aspects at once, including emotion, logic, reason, and spinning arguments. It's no small feat.

Takeaways:

- Negotiation is difficult, but that's mostly if you are only negotiating on one plane and not realizing that people have desires you can help fulfill. One of the keys of good negotiation is not only getting a good price, but also making both parties feel happy about getting some type of win.
- The foot in the door technique is helpful because you get to capitalize on people's tendency to drain willpower when they start with saying yes.
- The door in the face technique operates on the opposite principle—once you ask

for something huge initially, anything else you ask for will be deemed reasonable.

Chapter 6. How to Gain Trust and Credibility

Trust is tricky because almost everyone has a different definition of it. A notable difference is *how* people give trust to others.

Some people start with zero trust in strangers and keep their guards high until they see significant signs of trustworthiness and comfort. For these people, trust is slowly earned and a privilege, never a given. Trust is the ultimate placing of faith in someone, and that's not something to be taken lightly.

On the other hand, you have people who embrace strangers with open arms and assume good intentions and trustworthiness.

People only have to live up to this openness, and they are given the benefit of the doubt.

Wherever you might fall on that spectrum, it's clear that trust is assigned different values based on people's experiences. If you've had positive experiences with being open with strangers, you're more likely to continue in that fashion, and vice versa. But is there a way to shortcut the process if you come across someone who thinks trust is to be earned over a long period of time? How can you win over even the most guarded and standoffish person who doesn't even leave their bag with you when they use the restroom?

Festinger, Schachter, and Back studied the concept of trust in 1950. They studied people who lived in an apartment building and the patterns of the friendships that formed. They found that neighbors who were on the same floor tended to be friends, people who lived on different floors were rarely friends, and people who lived near the mailboxes and staircases were friends with people on different floors. What can we conclude from this?

To a large extent, friendship and trust increase *linearly* with simple interaction and exposure. The more we see someone, the more likely we will become friends with them and come to trust them. It didn't matter if there was any depth or rapport. This was dubbed *the Propinquity effect*.

The more we see people, the more we interact with them, the more similarities we find, the more comfort we build, and the more we find we can potentially like them. People cease to be stereotyped, two-dimensional characters and turn into unique humans. Prolonged exposure by itself will embed people into your mind as essentially part of the background. This is why when we change schools, jobs, or homes, we miss our neighbors or coworkers, even if we rarely spoke to them. There has been so much exposure and interaction that we tend to view them in a positive light and associate them with the environment as a whole. The level of interaction itself isn't important; the frequency of the interaction is.

The Propinquity effect is why it's not surprising that we are frequently friends with roommates, neighbors, coworkers, and classmates. You have a high level of exposure and interaction, you let your guard down around them, and you create an open mind toward friendship. If you look at your set of close friends, you would realize that a lot of those friends became friends of yours almost accidentally. They just frequently showed up in your life. They were at the right place at the right time and they did the same things you did. What does this mean for us?

Half of the battle in likability is *showing up* and not hiding in your room like a cat. The more you show your pretty face, the more trust will ultimately be built. For those you are specifically targeting to make friends and build trust with, make sure to frequently bump into them. The interaction itself can be minimal, as long as they take notice of your presence and acknowledge you. The goal is to become a known and familiar quantity in their lives.

This manifests in even tiny ways in our daily life. The more you see a certain barista at a café you frequent, the more you feel like you know and trust them. The more you see a neighbor, even if it's just while you are both taking out your trash, the more you feel like you understand who they are and trust them. Repetition creates trust.

Salespeople clearly use this to their advantage. A typical sales cycle depends on trust, because if a prospect doesn't trust the salesperson, they simply won't purchase. So what does a salesperson do? They become like white on rice. They are taught that the sale is made in the follow-up, and the Propinquity effect is part of the reason why.

They email, call, text, and make sure that you have so many points of contact with them that they are always in your ear. And oddly enough, this makes you trust them more because if they are that present in your life, and you have accepted this, they ought to be trustworthy, right? If we have multiple points of contact with people, we also begin to rationalize that they are indeed part of our lives—or should be.

If you are trying to get people to like you and become their friend, the same process applies. Obviously, adopt a subtler method, but it's undeniable how salespeople are able to gain our trust through repeated exposure and interaction.

Festinger proved that the whole key to trust is to simply show up. In the world of advertising, there is a fervent discussion on how many "touchpoints," or exposures, are required for a customer to buy a product. One of the most prevalent approaches, which has hazy origins in the 1930s movie industry, is that seven touchpoints are required: a marketing message has to be seen at least seven times for a purchase to occur. Another advertising guide written by Thomas Smith in 1885 espouses the need for 20 separate touchpoints before a purchase is made.

If you see an ad for a new soda, chances are you won't jump out of your seat to it the first time you see the ad. You would have to see the ad several times for you to feel the soda is legitimate. Only then is it worthy of becoming a potential choice. Then it has to compete with your other choices for soda, which requires additional touchpoints.

The Propinquity effect is highly related to the *mere exposure effect*, which similarly states the more we see something, the more we like it because we prefer familiarity. In 1968, researcher Robert Zajonc showed participants Chinese characters—some characters only once, and some up to 25 times. He asked them to guess the meaning of each character, and the more times a participant had been exposed to the Chinese character, the more positive of a meaning they assigned to it.

These two effects demonstrate that things tend to grow on us, and sometimes our tastes arise out of exposure, not free will. Familiarity is the ultimate precursor to trust.

Credibility can be seen as a higher degree of trust. If you trust someone, you believe them but may not be sure about their sense of judgment. However, if you believe someone has credibility, you may not necessarily trust them, but you view their judgment as rock-solid. You believe what they say, though you might feel differently about their character.

For instance, you trust your parents, but you aren't sure of their sense of judgment in the stock market. You may not trust your friend in finance, but they have higher credibility in making a judgment about the stock market. Both are important to likability.

Scientifically speaking, there is a wealth of subtle signs that can either bolster someone's credibility or tank it. If you've had any media training, or simply watched a politician interact with the media, you'll know that credibility doesn't just happen by accident. There are specific indicators that subconsciously signal that this person isn't a threat and in fact should be followed and listened to.

It's a finely tuned science that can make or break people. As recently as 1999, Gass and Selter sought to study credibility. They discovered a host of subtle indicators of credibility, as well as a host of signs that undermined credibility.

Here are the signs that need to be in play for people to think you're credible.

Highlight your experience and your qualifications. People are looking for an indication that you know what you're talking about. At the very least, they want to see facts that would support a conclusion that whatever judgments or decisions you make are based on something real. This is important for most people because if you've already seen something in the past, or have been educated about it, chances are you know the right things to do. You would have the right information so the right decisions are made. People want proven quantities and not just people making educated guesses.

Display how much you care. If it's obvious you care about other people and have their best interests at heart, they are more likely to trust you. You simply wouldn't act in any other way except to help them. However, if people can sense that you're looking to get a sale or line your own pockets, they are less likely to trust you. There is a conflict of interest here. They might feel that you are just too busy trying to benefit yourself instead of actually looking out for them. Don't show any ulterior motives, and let people know you are on their side.

Similarity. When people see that you are similar to them in terms of dress, body language, speaking style, and mother tongue, they are more likely to view you as credible. This should not be a surprise—in fact, there is an entire chapter devoted to this phenomenon already. People tend to like other people who are like them. This is especially true if it appears that you share the same values as the people you're trying to impress. They'll believe you because people automatically trust those similar to them, such as their family.

Appear assertive. If you are very assertive regarding your positions and you quickly and rationally destroy counterarguments, this makes you look like an expert. This is passion and conviction and confidence. This means that you know what you're talking about—or at least you look like you do. Chances are people can trust your judgments because you know the other side of the argument and can convincingly make those arguments go away. In other words, the more decisively you act, the more credible you appear.

Gain social proof. When other credible people recommend you, chances are people will be less suspicious of you. If people they know and trust as experts recommend you, then you are essentially riding on the coattails of those people. You don't have to convince people because people they trust already opened the doors for you. This is an extremely important competitive advantage. Unfortunately, not everybody can tap into this. This is what's behind every introduction. People will take a chance on you because someone vouched for you, and that's a powerful statement.

Likewise, there are certain signals you can send out that can erode your credibility.

Don't contradict yourself. If you are caught telling a lie or an obvious exaggeration, this can vaporize whatever credibility you've built up. If you're unsure about a certain assertion, follow this simple rule: when in doubt, leave it out. People may ask questions, and in many cases, you may not have answers to those questions. Instead of trying to look like a hero and guessing at an answer, you would be better off telling people you don't know or you'll get back to them. Recognize that you don't need an answer for everything, and if you appear infallible, it can look suspicious or manipulative. If you don't appear stupid, you might appear to be lying.

Avoid being overly polite. This might come as a surprise to some. By being excessively polite and brownnosing, you can come off as weak and tentative, which means that your opinions will also be taken as such. You look like you are simply looking for approval and telling people what they want to hear. You also appear to be insincere and manipulative, even if you are being sincere and honest. Too much politeness can often bely a lack of conviction or stance. You have to remember that people are looking for others whom they can listen to and follow. If you are busy walking on eggshells around them, you're sending the wrong signals.

When we apply for jobs, we make sure to include all of these factors and pay special attention to them. But credibility is just as important in the social arena, so it pays to be aware of what will subconsciously shift you into a person that others will seek to listen to. Credibility and trust work hand in hand in increasing your likability.

Takeaways:

- Trust has been shown to work on a linear

fashion. The more you see someone, the more you trust them, regardless of interaction or depth. This is known as the Propinquity effect, and it is similar to how studies have shown that customers only purchase after seeing a product seven times. It is also similar to the mere exposure effect.

- Credibility is a notch above trust, and there are also proven ways to generate that feeling. These include highlighting qualifications, showing your caring, showing similarity, being assertive, showing social proof, not contradicting yourself, and avoiding being overly polite.

Chapter 7. How to Work Well With Others

In an ideal world, the moment you become friends with somebody, they would instantly trust you and you would be in their inner circle.

But most friendships are tentative or probationary. You get put on some sort of outer circle of friendship until you prove yourself, at which point you get moved into an inner circle of intimacy. Other friendships are purely out of convenience, and both parties seem to know it. Sometimes we confuse acquaintances for friends and assume we are closer than we really are.

Whatever the case, it's clear people tend to create unofficial tiers of friends in their lives.

In the inner circle are your dearest friends and family members. In the circle further away from that are your other friends you might see four times a year. Outside of that circle might be your acquaintances, faded friendships, or business contacts you would only call upon if you had a clear reason to. Outside of that circle might be everyone else you know and don't devote any thought to at all.

Suppose people have those same four concentric circles of friends. It's clearly easy to get into the first two levels—and even the third level where you are a friend that is occasionally seen. But what about that elusive inner circle? How can you reach that level of friendship quickly and reliably with new and old friends?

It's not so simple. There are some hoops to jump through, and it's a process. In 1970, Bernard Murstein put forth one of the prevailing theories on friendship acquisition called the *stimulus-value-role model*.

The model describes the three stages of friendship, how we select the people that inhabit each stage, and what is required for someone to make it to your inner circle. There are specific elements that are important at each stage but may lose relative importance for deeper stages of friendship and relationships overall. The three stages act as a series of gates: only if you pass one gate are you granted passage to the next. If you understand which stage you're currently in, you'll be able to move ahead more easily because you'll know what you need to do.

The first stage of friendship is the *stimulus stage*, and in this stage of friendship we are primarily concerned with evaluating people based on their physical attributes and superficial traits. Think of this stage like the *eye test*—if by looking at two people you would assume they are friends, that's the standard people subconsciously use. We seek people who are attractive but also of a similar age, appearance, and perception of status.

This stage of friendship is shallow and is more about whom we *want* to be friends with. If an impoverished 90-year-old is close friends with a rich 20-year-old, we would consider this an unlikely friendship because it doesn't appear to pass the stimulus stage. Often, if someone doesn't fit into the stimulus stage, we will never pursue a friendship with them because it seems too unlikely. We just dismiss people as "not our type" and move on with hardly a second thought.

The second stage of friendship is the *value stage*, and in this stage, we are concerned with finding people that share our thoughts and morals. We are seeking people with similar worldviews and senses of right and wrong. In essence, compatibility is the main emphasis here. For an extreme example of a group that concerns itself highly with the value stage, look no further than the *Ku Klux Klan* (the KKK)—it is built upon a specific set of beliefs that bonds it together. We are similarly looking for people who think like us and whom we can ultimately relate to. We might tolerate being acquaintances with someone who possess a belief that is vile to us, but we will never be good friends with them. The more similar values line up, the more there is to discuss and bond over.

The final and deepest stage of friendship, the inner circle, is the *role stage*. This stage of friendship is based on how people will complement us in working toward a shared goal. This means the deepest friendships function in a sense like business relationships—there has to be ultimate compatibility and a sense of benefit for each party. There has to be a willingness of roles, duties, and obligations and an implicit understanding of the terms of engagement. People understand each other, help with weaknesses, and utilize each other in a beneficial manner. You can work out conflict and generally be compatible in tough situations.

Think about how a couple must learn to resolve conflict peacefully and come to an agreement on budgeting and finances. These are all ways in which a working relationship is necessary to be fully compatible for the inner circle. Could you be friends with someone who never cleaned up your shared apartment if you were obsessive about being clean? The jury is out on that one.

These are three distinct phases of how people learn to value you as a friend. To gain access to the inner circle, it is important to know where you stand and what stage you should be trying to fulfill.

People filter their contacts on a subconscious level. Simply by being aware that this subconscious filtering process is taking place, you can put yourself in a better position and send out specifically desired behaviors and signals to move through the three stages sooner rather than later. Now that you know which factors are immediately important in becoming good friends with someone, you can change your actions and emphasize different aspects of your personality to seamlessly flow from stage one to stage three.

Let's suppose you want to befriend John, an enthusiastic soccer fan.

To gain entry into the first stage, your task would be to appear as if you belong. As I mentioned, if someone took a picture of you two together, would it appear that you would be friends? At the outset, it would be beneficial to wear a soccer jersey and emulate his general style and appearance. First, look the part, and John will be open to you.

Next, your task would be to gently and subtly probe for John's values about the world, what he sees as right and wrong, and his general life philosophy. You want to present yourself as having the same morals and values as him, regardless of your background or pedigree.

At this stage, you have shown yourself to look and act the part. Finally, to enter the inner circle and pass into the role stage, you would want to show that you share similar activities and you possess the ability to work together without any conflict.

Meeting up for lunch or coffee doesn't forge a deep relationship—going through a trial by fire does. There's a saying that you don't know anyone until you attempt to travel together, and the role stage is exactly what's meant by that.

If you can travel together, which involves a huge amount of planning and execution, then you have shown compatibility and chemistry on a far deeper level. Spending time together as friends will be a snap. If during the planning you differ on too many aspects and argue, you probably aren't going to pass the role stage. But if you can successfully plan together and navigate conflict, which are no small feats, you are well on your way to the inner circle and mutual respect.

The role stage means that you can function and actually work together. Not coincidentally, this is why a lot of business deals get done on the golf course and on bar napkins—people are able to decide that they can work with each other's reciprocal abilities and move into each other's inner circle.

The three stages of the stimulus-value-role model of friendship are important to understanding how you should act with people. It may start with simple physical mirroring or attraction, but it ends with the ability to coexist on multiple levels. The ability to work together is an important factor in likability, and this was also investigated by Stephen Deberry in 1989.

Deberry split participants into groups of two and filled out a scale of likability about themselves and their partner. Then the participants either completed a task involving blocks with help from their partner or individually and in competition with their partner. After the task, the participants filled out the likability scale once again for both people.

Deberry discovered a difference in how genders perceived collaborating and competing. Collaborating females liked their partners more than competing females; this effect was only found in females. Females in competitive groups ranked themselves much lower in terms of likability after the task. Males in competitive groups ranked themselves much higher in the competitive tasks.

What the results seemed to imply was that females are less competitive and more collaborative in nature than males, and when they are forced to compete, their self-image takes a hit. Males, on the other hand, are more competitive and their self-image doesn't take a hit when they're put in a competitive environment. Avoid competition when working with women, but be aware that competition can drive males to achieve and feel good about themselves.

Be aware of this gender divide when you are conversing with or working with another person.

The key takeaway to this research is to avoid competition and comparison in social settings, unless you know the outcome will make the other person feel better about themselves. In other words, bringing up your massive salary can make people feel inadequate. However, you can certainly feel free to bring up your salary if you have a good inkling the other person's salary will be higher than or at least comparable to yours. Downplay anything you think people might feel compelled to make comparisons with.

When you are working together, focus on the shared goal at hand and not individual contributions. Everything is equal in pursuit of the goal; you don't want to trigger the negative consequences of competition.

As for likability? When people see you as an ally, or as somebody who could help them at some level or another, they are more likely to view you favorably. At the very least, they're not going to see you as a threat. Now, if you were to talk to people and you're constantly comparing scores, income, net worth, social status, social esteem, authority, credibility, and so on and so forth, you're going to trigger their competitive nature.

This is difficult for some because it requires that you get over your ego—yes, even in the work context.

Remember that the overarching goal of any interaction, whether social or work-related, is not to look good by crushing another person. Your overarching goal should be to build rapport and comfort, and in this chapter, specifically to showcase the traits and values that will move you through people's friendship stages. You can make the argument this chapter is more about the value of being able to work well with others. The important part is to recognize the working relationship as an integral part of any close friendship.

Takeaways:

- The stimulus-value-role model of social interaction states that to get to someone's inner circle, you have to show three levels of compatibility: stimulus, value, and role. To use this model, you have to first understand which stage you are currently at with someone, and then you can understand what you need to get into the next stage. The deepest level is role: working together, collaborating, and resolving conflict.

- Within working together successfully, there is a gender divide where males are more comfortable with competition and comparison. However, no matter who you are working with, people will favor you if you can make them feel good about themselves.

Chapter 8. How to Be More Endearing

How would you act if the most stunningly attractive and physically perfect person suddenly sat down next to you?

If you were at home, you might tell them to get out of your house. But otherwise, we would likely be reduced to a stuttering mess. There's a very simple reason for this: perfect people scare and intimidate us.

We're uncomfortable around them, and they make us self-conscious in ways we never thought possible. It's impossible to not compare yourself to a supermodel who sits down next to you, no matter your gender, and it's *near*-impossible to not feel intensely intimidated or paralyzed if a supermodel was to sit down in front of you and proclaim their interest in you. A person without flaws just seems superhuman, and it can generate a sense of shock and wonder as you think, "Are we even the same species?"

They seem unrelatable and like engaging with you would be *below* them. Okay, that might be a little hyperbolic, but the fact of the matter is that perfection and flawlessness are not wholly positive traits.

To illustrate this concept, in recent years there has been an exponentially greater number of media and movies about Batman and Spider-Man over Superman. Let's suppose we can use this as a proxy for how popular each superhero is. Why might Batman and Spider-Man be more popular than Superman?

I have my own theory. Superman is literally, well, a super man. He has no weaknesses beyond a rare type of rock. Most of his struggles, if we take a step back and think, can be solved with a single punch because he can lift a house effortlessly. He is rarely actually challenged, and it takes considerable work to make him vulnerable. There are only so many times Superman can be exposed to kryptonite before the audience groans and just begs him to get a radiation-proof spandex suit.

Batman and Spider-Man, on the other hand, are powerful yet deeply vulnerable characters. They're not invulnerable, and they can be killed by a normal knife or gun. Most importantly, they are extremely flawed characters who are superheroes because of their own internal struggles. Batman's parents were killed in front of him when he was a child (something that every movie inexplicably feels the need to recreate), and Spider-Man's uncle was killed by a criminal he could have stopped. They are driven by guilt, purpose, anger, and frustration.

Coincidentally, these are extremely humanizing characteristics that make them far more relatable (and thus popular) to us than Superman. People are moved to *feel* for Spider-Man and Batman because they can also point to their own internal battles and how they've overcome them or not. They are compelling precisely because they aren't perfect.

What does this have to do with the science of likability? *Not* being perfect is endearing to people. Vulnerability is attractive and relatable, and it ensures that you aren't intimidating to others. Don't pretend you're perfect—you're not, anyway—because it will probably backfire on you.

In fact, consciously display the opposite.

Aronson, Willerman, and Floyd in 1966 discovered an easy way to create likability that capitalized on displaying imperfection. The researchers ran a simple experiment where participants watched a video of a person knocking a cup of coffee over and a video of another person *not* knocking the cup of coffee over.

The results? It was shown that participants highly preferred and liked the person who had knocked the cup of coffee over. In essence, it was found that flaws, hiccups, and imperfections that showed people to be vulnerable made people likable. This was called the *Pratfall effect*, presumably named after someone named Prat who had a tendency to fall frequently. (In actuality, it's an antiquated name for the act of someone falling onto their buttocks.)

When we display imperfection, we appear more approachable and relatable—overall more *human*. The more important, unspoken element of showing flaws Is that you are making others comfortable and easing their fear of judgment. That's one of the reasons we are really uncomfortable around perfection—because we feel we will be judged and inevitably come up short. If we're around someone amazingly charismatic and loud, we might walk on eggshells and not say anything out of fear that it pales in comparison to them.

If we're around someone amazingly beautiful, we might hide our faces or intentionally dress sloppily so as not to be compared to them. If we're around someone shockingly intelligent, we might not want to voice our opinions for fear of being found wrong and humiliated. You haven't done anything wrong, but people's insecurities can easily get the best of them.

But when you commit a silly error, show a chink in your armor, or overall destroy any mystique people might have about you, that all changes. You become human and more likable. People know you're not a living statue or encyclopedia, and they will feel they don't have to walk on eggshells around you anymore because you're just like them. Any self-consciousness will evaporate if the supposed genius has a tendency to spill coffee on her pants or the piano prodigy chipped his tooth while drinking coffee too aggressively. People won't be so concerned with how they appear, and they will *relax*.

Suddenly, you will become the substitute teacher who swears in front of their students in the first five minutes of class—the class will relax because they previously felt like they had to be on their best behavior, and now they know their substitute teacher is actually going to be lenient and relaxed.

If you have a quirk or eccentricity, it is probably the reason why a lot of your friends are drawn to you. Your value to your friends definitely doesn't come from a place of perfection. They like you because of your imperfections and what makes you uniquely you. In fact, you probably have imperfections or quirks in common, and that's what drew you to each other in the first place. Politicians around the world are aware of the effect humanization can have on their popularity, which is why you'll see them dress-down and intentionally use the language of the average Joe or Jane.

This chapter is a long way of saying I'd feel a lot more comfortable around Heidi Klum if she tripped and fell on her face to break her facade of being a beautiful Amazonian model. How can you use this knowledge in your daily life to be more likable?

There are any number of ways to make your appearance slightly goofier and less polished, which we know makes us a bit more endearing to others.

For example, you can stumble a bit when you use stairs, exaggerate a yawn, wrinkle and rub your nose, drop something you're carrying, snort while you laugh, walk into the corner of a table or door, drive onto a curb while parallel parking, stub your toe, get hit by a tree branch while walking, etc. The list is endless.

You can also make self-deprecating jokes and immediately call yourself out when you have made a mistake. Finally, you can make sure to freely bring up or admit embarrassing things about yourself, such as your past love affair with ice cream or that you broke your leg chasing an ice cream truck.

Typically, these are acts or thoughts we seek to hide as quickly as possible. But they actually make you more likable and endearing because they allow others to let go of their insecurities and let their guards down. I imagine having to conform to perfection as sitting in perfect posture on an uncomfortable chair made out of splintered wood. Why do that when you can slouch into a worn leather couch and kick your feet up?

Another trait that will make you more endearing is the ability to deliver bad news in a good way. No one likes to hear bad news, and often we take it out on the messenger. What if you are forced to be that messenger?

You're stuck between a rock and a hard place, unless you can harness what is known as *the Losada ratio*.

The Losada ratio is the ratio of how much positive feedback is required to lessen the sting of negative feedback. In a 2004 study, Marcial Losada studied communications within a set of businesses to examine the relationship between positivity and performance. He found that a greater amount of positivity was highly correlated to better performance and higher rates of success, especially in the presence of negativity.

Even positive statements as simple as "I agree with you" or "That's a good idea" were highly important to curtailing the effects of negative statements as simple as "I disagree" or "I don't think that's a good idea." Losada discovered the amount of positivity it took to reduce the impact from negativity was roughly 5.6:1—which means in order to make someone feel good about any amount of negative or critical feedback, you need to make six positive statements to maintain a healthy work relationship. Otherwise, the negative impact on someone's self-esteem and mood will be damaged—not irreparably, but in a way that may impact the future relationship.

Teams that tended to produce better work and get along better with each other learned that positivity goes a long way. The best-performing teams averaged 5.6 positive comments for every one negative comment. Team members within these teams showed a higher level of likability to each other.

How can you use this finding to your advantage? If you want to be likable, load up on positive statements during the course of the conversation—especially if you know you're going to have to deliver anything remotely negative. It's the art of *sugarcoating* when you know you need to go negative.

In every conversation, there are three types of statements: neutral, positive, and negative. Be aware of the type of statement that you are using and police what's coming out of your mouth. If you know you have to deliver a negative statement, make sure to use the bulk of the positivity afterward, because only then will you be directly counteracting the effects of the negativity. Be sure it is actually positive and not simply neutral.

For instance, you can heap praise on someone and then conclude that their presentation needed work. The praise will likely be forgotten by the impact of the negativity. If you reverse the order and lead with the negativity, the positivity will blunt the impact. It's tough to keep track of 5.6:1 positive to negative statements in real life, so you don't need to seek exact application here. You just need to realize the massive effect that negativity can have and understand the steps you can take to counteract it.

It's not only supervisors or people who critique and judge others on a daily basis who need to understand this. In social settings, we also unintentionally use negativity more than we think—from disagreeing on the choice of restaurant to eat at, to making fun of someone's new haircut. This includes the use of sarcasm, which for the purposes of the Losada ratio is typically negative, even if it used in good humor.

People are more sensitive than they present themselves to be, and you can choose to acknowledge this or not. You don't have to compliment people and act like a sycophant—

just erring on the side of positive and good-natured will do quite a bit of good. Shooting for 5.6:1 does seem impossibly tough and transparent, but if you were able to alter your statements at least halfway, there would be a world of difference.

The final specific way to be more endearing and enjoyable is to ask people for advice and revere them as experts.

In a 2015 study (Brooks, Gino, Schweitzer), researchers separated a group of participants into two halves. The first half was paid $1 for each test question they answered correctly, while the second half was paid based on how competent their partner rated them. Before completing the test questions, participants had the option to send a message to their partner. The message could be either asking for advice or merely wishing them luck with the questions. Afterward, the participants were polled on how much they liked their partner.

What ended up happening was participants who were asked for their partner's advice rated their partner higher on competence and also reported liking them quite a bit more than participants who only wished their partner good luck. This study found a positive correlation between the impression we have on somebody and whether they asked us for advice.

When someone asks us for advice, it's hard to resist stepping onto a soapbox and educating. When someone puts you in a position of expertise and asks you to help them, it is difficult to resist the temptation of telling them *everything* we know about the topic. Let's imagine you have just come back from a skiing trip, and someone asks you if you know any good places to ski. They have no idea you're essentially an expert on the topic at the moment because you planned the trip yourself.

What is your response most likely going to be?

You are going to tell them absolutely everything about your trip, send them your itinerary, talk about the various pros and cons of your particular trip, and offer any other advice you can think of. You're going to feel smart because you have the ability to guide and teach someone. It's important to mention this doesn't tend to occur because we are innately helpful and generous with our time; it tends to occur because we enjoy feeling validated and important.

To be more endearing, make other people experts and ask them for their advice—even if you don't need it. On an everyday level, this can display itself as more curiosity about topics another person has knowledge about. What does the person like to do? What are their hobbies? What is their educational background, or what do they have special training in? All of us have areas of interest, and we would welcome it when people ask us about stuff that we're interested in. A bit of recognition, enthusiasm, and curiosity directed toward it feels great.

If someone is a Renaissance fair enthusiast, you could ask them specific questions about how they function and what's involved in attending one. Make sure to ask for advice regarding them, not just logistical or broad questions. Advice sounds more like, "How can I do that?" versus "So what do you wear?"

We love displaying our deeper thoughts on a topic of expertise, something we almost never get the chance to do. Most of us may not seek out the spotlight willingly, but if someone else shines it onto us, we will gladly seize it for a brief amount of time because it makes us feel smart. This ties to the central fact that people love to talk about themselves. *You* are the sole topic that occupies your mind the vast majority of the time; people are selfish by nature.

Asking advice of others is not necessarily about extracting information. The main benefit here is not learning where the best ski slopes are; it is to help the other person feel good about themselves and increase the comfort they feel with you. Of course, that leads directly to greater likability.

Takeaways:

- One of the easiest ways to be endearing is to stop trying to be perfect and impressive. Instead, try to be relatable and harmless to a degree. Nothing epitomizes that better than the Pratfall effect, which shows the attractiveness of imperfection and vulnerability. This also works because you are catering to people's insecurities and allowing them to feel that judgment is not imminent.
- Another aspect of being endearing is to make rough times better, which is possible through using the Losada ratio. This ratio should govern the amount of positive and negative remarks you use—roughly five positive to make up for one negative.
- Finally, you can be endearing if you make other people feel like experts and ask them questions they feel they are specially equipped to answer.

Chapter 9. How to Convince People to Act

I occasionally babysit a friend's toddler. Her name is Aria, but her mother insists it has nothing to do with *Game of Thrones* or the popstar Rihanna. Apparently she was named for the type of song, but I have my doubts.

The part of the day we both dread most is bedtime. I dread it because I know it's going to be an eternal struggle to get her into bed without having to chase her around, and she dreads it because she wants to stay up late to watch violent television.

Aria's mother let me in on a tip she discovered long ago—it wasn't necessarily that Aria hated bedtime and sleeping. She actually quite enjoyed being tucked in and being read to. Who doesn't? What she hated was listening to instruction from anyone. If I told her to do something she loved, like eat pie, she would refuse. She just didn't like being told what to do, and there was something inside her brain that told her to resist and do the opposite.

You might see where I'm going with this.

The next time I babysat, I said something I felt would be far too obvious, even to a toddler. I told her, "Okay, you're not allowed to get ready for bed. It's against the rules!" She gave me a look of defiance and ran toward the bathroom and started brushing her teeth immediately. I followed her and pretended to protest, and she was in her bed in record time.

Does this type of reverse psychology only work on children? Well, unfortunately, no. It's in our nature to resist and try to claim our free will as adults as well. Statements as transparent as the ones that worked on Aria might not work on us, but it doesn't take much more complexity to convince people to act in just the way you want.

If we want to get something done, we might feel that we need to be direct in a way that makes us unlikable—even if we use the Losada ratio. This chapter just might reveal a way to accomplish your goals while still being likable and not ruffling anyone's feathers. *Reactance theory* may help you assert a level of influence by taking advantage of human nature while maintaining any and all positive feelings.

Reactance theory originated from Jack Brehm in 1966. It is a theory that dictates how humans behave when they feel their free will or freedom is being threatened. This is what Aria felt when she was told she couldn't do something—her free will to do whatever she wanted was being threatened, so she followed reactance theory perfectly by wanting to reclaim her freedom and display it. Humans will bristle when their perceived freedom is restricted, so they'll try to reclaim it. It is similar to reverse psychology, but reverse psychology is driven by the question, "What am I missing out on?"

In other words, if we are told we can't do something, we immediately want to do it— not because of the action itself, but because we feel psychological discomfort with being told we can't do something, and we seek to prove to ourselves that we indeed can. We will probably want to perform that action more if we are told we can't do it because it will have greater psychological and emotional value at that point.

So for instance, if you are told you can't buy something, you are likely to feel slighted and annoyed at the fact someone told you this. You might even feel insulted or controlled. All of these emotions lead to you buying something you may not want just to resolve those negative feelings inside you and be able to say, "Ha, I showed them!"

We can accept some restrictions on our

freedom. We abide by them all the time, from crossing the street at red lights to not stealing. The difference is these are universally applied and generally appear to be reasonable and fair. Reactance theory kicks in most powerfully when we feel we our freedom is unfairly, arbitrarily, or unreasonably restricted—in our perception.

Reactance theory shows an interesting aspect of the human desire for choice and options. Choice and options give us the feeling that we can control what happens in our lives.

In 1976, Pennebaker and Sanders studied reactance and illustrated it in a somewhat humorous way. They didn't give instruction to participants directly. Instead, they put two types of signs up in bathrooms. One sign read, "Do not write on these walls under any circumstances," while the other sign contained no such language.

Can you guess what happened?

The signs with language specifically

prohibiting writing were covered with graffiti, while the normal signs had far less or none at all. What people were specifically told to avoid, they did to satiate an impulse they had about their freedom. I imagine the inner monologue of someone who came across that sign was something like, "Oh yeah? Stupid sign creator trying to tell me what to do? I'll show them…" It may sound immature, but it was a textbook instance of a seemingly unreasonable restriction on free will that caused people to demonstrate their free will.

There probably weren't many graffiti artists in the area, but the people who drew on the signs just wanted to feel that they could without anyone running into the bathroom and arresting them. They had the power, and they weren't going to be told what to do by a *sign*.

Reactance theory might also be behind one of literature's greatest love stories: *Romeo and Juliet*. How else might teenagers act if they were explicitly told to not see someone because their families were feuding?

Whatever the case, reactance theory is more commonly utilized as reverse psychology. Tell people to do something, and intend for them to do the opposite. Tell Aria she can't sleep, and watch her to do the opposite. Tell Mike he can't possibly buy that shirt, and he probably will. Tell your significant other they are forbidden from looking inside your desk, and they *definitely* will.

Knowing this is the case, you can convince people to do what you want by insinuating they don't have the freedom to do the opposite. Specifically, if you want action X, you can insinuate any of the following:

- They can't do X.
- They are forbidden from doing X.
- They are incapable of doing X.
- They aren't allowed to do X.
- They can't handle X.
- Trust me, you don't want to do X.
- X isn't for people like you.

How would you react to any of those subtle

jabs? I can guarantee you wouldn't agree outright, and there would absolutely be varying degrees of resistance, annoyance, and anger. This is reactance theory in a nutshell. We can be spiteful creatures from time to time. It also capitalizes on other aspects of human nature, such as curiosity, excitement about forbidden fruit, and rising to meet a challenge.

For some, this chapter might sound a bit unnecessary and immature, but there are simply times when making a direct request to people doesn't work. Again, it's almost never about the action or behavior—it's about how people feel being told to do something.

We hate it. Thus, this is something we have to work around. This is especially true for people who are innately resistant to change and act stubbornly. You probably won't win with a direct request, because you will immediately start to butt heads with them. Aria's mother warned me of this—if you push her too hard on anything, she will rebel and do the opposite. There's certainly a fine line where reactance theory can work.

Reactance theory is a strong reflection of how much people value their freedom of choice. In limited instances, you can indeed use this drive against them.

Takeaways:

- Reverse psychology works on children, and the slightly more advanced form, reactance theory, works on adults. Reactance theory is when you can subtly push people in a direction you want because they feel that you are trying to restrict their free will regarding it.
- The important factor is that someone feels like they are being restricted in a way that is unfair and arbitrary, which leads to psychological discomfort.

Chapter 10. How to Lead Anyone

Have you ever heard of a famous and successful company led by a committee of CEOs? A country with two presidents?

We never hear about anything being led by a group of people. There Is a reason there is one head of state for every country in the world. There is only one president or prime minister because there needs to be a singular person making decisions and having the last word on matters. There needs to be a tie-breaker and figurehead people can rally behind. Other times, there is simply one person who knows better than everyone else.

Organizations have leaders, and we sometimes instinctually look for leaders to take cues from in all walks of life. We don't come out and admit it, but we are often looking to be led and for someone to make decisions for us. A shepherd is a valuable and comforting presence. It's also less brainwork to follow and not make decisions—as long as you trust who is making them for you.

Sometimes we want the supreme freedom of choice you read about in the previous chapter, but other times, we just want to be told what to do. Sometimes we have surprising clarity about what we know and don't know and rely upon others to provide guidance and direction. This occurs mostly when we feel unconfident about our own intuitions or we believe someone to possess better judgment than us.

This is true even when it comes to emotions—don't your friends ask you your opinion on their love lives, and whether or not they are justified in their reactions?

Every friend group has an unofficial leader, someone people will look to whenever there is a decision or plan to be made. A natural hierarchy will always form, and it's your decision as to whether you want to be on the top of the pyramid or someone who will simply follow the path set out for them.

Leadership isn't a skill you're just magically born with. In a vacuum, leadership is simply about convincing people to listen to you. There are many ways we can do this that aren't the stereotype of King Leonidas commanding his 300 Spartan warriors. It's easier than you think to step into the leadership role among your friends or at work, because there are many ways to accomplish the goal of getting people to listen.

Most people who struggle with leadership aren't finding the most effective way to get people to listen. Daniel Goleman, in a seminal study of over 3000 managers conducted in 2000, articulated six distinct leadership styles and types. Which of these types is best suited toward your personality, and which should you absolutely stay away from?

Each type of leader caters to a different type of intelligence and primary motivator—after all, not all of us are motivated or driven in the same ways. And of course, these all speak to ways we can get people behind us and win their support. The six types of leaders are:

1. Visionary: "Come with me to a better world."
2. Coaching: "Try this, and you might learn from it."
3. Affiliate: "Only if everyone feels good about it."
4. Democratic: "What does everyone think?"
5. Pace-setting: "Do more faster."
6. Commanding: "Do what I say."

Unsurprisingly, different people have different needs and respond to different kicks in the behind. Placing people into one of the six categories can help you skyrocket your effectiveness as a leader. The round hole gets the round peg, and the square hole gets the square peg—and the benefits are limitless.

Visionary Leader

The visionary leader is someone who motivates because they can speak to people's desire to be part of something bigger than themselves. They move people toward an overall vision and purpose. The visionary leader emphasizes the brave, new world they want to help create.

This type of leader drives others toward a shared vision. This shared vision is, of course, an ideal. This leader tells the group about the vision they should all share but doesn't necessarily lead by telling them how to get there. This type of leadership is more abstract and motivational in setting priorities.

This type of emotional leadership is powerful because laying out a vision enables people to coordinate by sharing information and also puts them in a position to motivate each other as they struggle toward that goal.

This is where leaders like Nelson Mandela or Martin Luther King, Jr. come into play. They were charismatic, fierce leaders in their own right, but they rallied people to a greater cause—a vision for worlds that were free of discrimination and segregation, a world that was based on equality and free will. They persuaded people this was a vision worth aiming toward and brought it into reality.

A drawback of the visionary leader is they may fall short when trying to motivate those who have different overall visions, even if they only differ by a little bit. Then you might fall into a battle of visions where you don't necessarily want different things, but people are sticking by their individual principles. In any case, it's more productive to invite everyone to share views and take a seat at the table so you can tailor your vision to be all-inclusive. Get them to feel that they have "skin in the game" by working with them to fit their existing experience and vision to the grand vision you have in mind.

If your group has tried a lot of different

methods to get inspired and moving, a visionary approach can be extremely effective because it is emotional in nature. It will focus people and have a strong impact on the climate surrounding your team.

In practical terms, this emotional leadership approach works best when you're dealing with people who are looking to fill a gap or void. They have energy and they have passion, but they feel unfulfilled or untapped. This person is looking for direction and would be very open minded to ideas and directions you have. A grand vision just might be the inspiration they need for you to take lead.

Coaching Leader

The coaching leader is focused on individuals instead of an overarching vision or goal. Of course, it's best if individual development can line up with something grander, but it's not imperative.

The coaching leader is more of a facilitator. This person connects personal wants of team members to the goals of a particular group. What does each individual want in a group, organization, company, or context?

The coaching leader tries to deliver it to them so they feel they are working toward something they specifically want. Understandably, this is motivating because it allows people to feel selfish in an acceptable way. They will help team members dig deep within themselves to identify weaknesses and strengths and how these can tie into their personal and group goals.

The coaching leader is best exemplified by, you guessed it, a coach. A football coach is focused on improving the skills of each individual player so they can contribute to the team's success as a whole. The individual player feels compelled to follow the instruction because they trust the coach's abilities and knowledge, and the coach is motivated by improving the components of his team.

A coaching leader often produces a high

degree of loyalty because people have a sense of how much their improvement and accomplishments are due to this leader.

The drawback is they can easily come off as micromanaging. By digging so deeply into the personal lives of your friends and coworkers, it may seem like you are prying or directing people regarding minute life details. It is too easy to be misunderstood as a busybody or "know it all" when this type of leadership is unwelcome or changes a relationship dynamic.

If you're dealing with people who are a long way off from reaching their full capabilities, a coaching leadership style works great. It's useful for growth and maturation.

Affiliative Leader

Affiliative leaders emphasize interpersonal relationships and emotional needs. This is a person who tries to get all team members or friends more deeply connected with each other. The hope is once these connections are made, people will collaborate because they have become emotionally invested in the people around them. Instead of fervently working toward an overarching goal, people will be inspired to fervently work to not let each other down and to make each other proud.

The affiliate leader makes people open up instead of necessarily getting things done directly.

A clear illustration of the affiliative leader is a couple's counselor. In couple's counseling, the main goal is often to be able to hear your partner clearly and understand what they want. The counselor doesn't have to do much besides interpret answers and ask the right questions. In doing so, the counselor allows the couple to find themselves and work together out of love and respect.

When performing poorly, the affiliative leader doesn't illuminate and ignores the realities in front of them. There can be such a focus on making people feel good and interconnected that negative yet crucial feedback is swept under the rug. All aspects, positive and negative, must be exposed for people to understand each other better. An affiliative leader can be seen more like the head of a family. They create emotional buy-in and investment above all else.

Democratic Leader

The method is in the name. The democratic leader seeks to build consensus through a process that includes all the parties present. When you feel like you've had a say in the matter, you suddenly feel investment and interest in reaching your goals. In a sense, the democratic leader is less of a leader and more of an organizer or administrator. They do not make decisions themselves, but they synthesize the information and present it to others so they may make the best decisions.

This person works to get as many different inputs as possible from team members. They're not seeking a specific answer. Instead, the focus is on simply getting people to participate by sharing their point of view. Democratic leaders ask intelligent questions and listen for the subtext when people answer.

Examples of pure democratic leaders exist in groups where both sides are presented information and then the majority rules. This exists in various types of legislative or parliamentary bodies. Allow the groups to make their arguments, moderate the discussion or debate, and then move matters along so a resolution may be made.

When people share, they care. A huge benefit of democratic leaders is to involve others directly in making decisions, which makes them substantially more passionate. People don't like to feel like they've wasted their time, even by just voicing their opinion or making an argument. They share because they want to get certain things done.

The democratic leader is best if highly organized and adept at gathering information and presenting it to others. Just be cautious you aren't creating more problems than you are solving.

Pace-Setting Leader

The pace-setting leader is all about milestones, deliverables, and performance.

They are often the people installed as CEOs of companies that want to ramp up their growth because they know the metrics to focus attention on. This leader shows a high amount of ambition and makes everyone else adapt to their high standards.

They will challenge, prod, and even offend if things aren't up to par. But everything Is for the sake of the team's accomplishments. Often, the pace-setting leader has done these things themselves and is leading by stellar example, which also pushes the standards for excellence. These leaders exemplify their standards. They show people how to get stuff done because they live out their own goals. They are role models to aspire to.

They know that people who are under-achieving aren't necessarily incapable. By sitting people down, demanding more of them, and offering to work with them, they motivate them to get going. But this won't happen often.

The most common downside to this type of emotional leadership is that it tends to be light on guidance and high on metrics and deliverables. There just isn't the time for coaching or teaching, and it can produce a pressure-cooker environment. This leader might just tell them that they need to get their act together—if they can't, then it's onto the next person who can. You set up a destination and you expect them to instinctively know how to get there. It can be cutthroat.

Bad usage of this leadership style betrays a lack of emotional intelligence and compassion. In many cases, being an overly pace-setting, emotional leader may make you look like you don't have much self-management or self-control skills. You may appear tone deaf.

Thus, the pace-setting leader works best when dealing with people who are already competent and motivated. They are capable and just need a push to take them to the next level.

However, if you're dealing with people who aren't motivated or capable, the pace-setting leader is almost a waste because their main value can't be used. They can take an organization from a 7 to a 10, but not necessarily from a 3 to a 7.

In the short-term, this can produce a lot of tension and pain as people see they need to change their habits and behavior, but it's all for the long-term benefits and accomplishments.

Commanding Leader

The commanding leader is a leader through and through. They expect to be listened to, and they speak in the cadence of commands and orders. They use compliance to get through tough times and motivate people through fear or intimidation.

This is not a style of leadership that everyone can adopt. It requires degrees of emotional separation and discipline because you essentially have to see others as your tools. It's easy to come off as cold, distant, and uncaring. Some people will respond to this, while others will balk at the lack of emotional investment.

The commanding leader really shines in one particular circumstance: hardship. When a team or organization is going through a crisis, the commanding leader can jump in, seize the reins, and single-handedly right the ship with rapid action. Consider why the army and military are so intentional about breaking their recruits down. It is so they can command absolute compliance and get them to do things like march into gunfire. The commanding leader sees the overall picture and can make difficult decisions and handle confrontation others may not be able to.

When you really need something done, this is the type of leadership everyone will resort to on some level. Barking commands and curt words are the hallmark of tense times.

Suffice it to say, this is a leadership style that should be a last resort or used sparingly. If done poorly, it can cause more problems than it solves and ruffle the feathers or everyone around you. In the short-term, this can be a great solution to reaching goals. However, long-term, this wlll wear on anyone and it isn't sustainable. It ignores people's emotional needs, and that's a terrible management strategy.

It must be noted that Goleman's study also found that the most successful of the 3000 managers he studied were able to blend different leadership styles and calibrate the styles to different circumstances. In other words, they were able to roll with the punches and adapt their style to what they saw was necessary at the time and what their employees needed at the time.

Likewise, by understanding the six leadership styles, you can position yourself with the tools to approach any type of person or situation. Different people have different needs. These needs and preferences often change with time. You can either adapt to this or become an ineffectual leader.

This obviously makes you not just likable, but also, in many cases, emotionally indispensable. People will feel that you're speaking their exact language when, in reality, you understand six different types of needs people will frequently have. You become more likable with an approach that mirrors and resonates with your personality, so do a bit of introspection and decide how to approach others.

Takeaways:

- There are six types of leadership, and it's up to you to discover which suits you best and is most effective in your context.
- Visionary: "Come with me to a better

world."

- Coaching: "Try this, and you might learn from it."
- Affiliate: "Only if everyone feels good about it."
- Democratic: "What does everyone think?"
- Pace-setting: "Do more faster."
- Commanding: "Do what I say."

Chapter 11. How to Avoid Being Judged

One of the most common fears that keep us from doing what we want is the fear of judgment.

We are perpetually concerned with what others think about us. We never want to make a bad impression, and the worst thing that could possibly happen is to have people think we're stupid.

If we catch even a whiff that this is occurring, we imagine the world is ending and that we will become a social pariah. One wrong word and that's all it takes. This is what goes through the minds of people with low self-confidence. They're petrified of judgment and rejection and will go to great lengths to avoid it.

How can the science of likability shield us from feeling negatively judged? It begins with *how* people tend to form stereotypes about others. The less knowledge we have about someone, the more we judge them because we have the tendency to fill in the blanks with information that is largely drawn from stereotypes. This has largely been beneficial for us in wilder times in the quest to avoid predators and rotten fruit, but it may not apply as readily to social situations.

For example, if you hear about someone who plays tennis and belongs to a country club, what other pieces of information fit into a view of that person? You would likely assume they were rich growing up, perhaps owned a boat, lived on an estate, went to a fancy private school, and haven't had to work very hard in their life. Maybe not all, but at least a couple of those things sprang into your mind.

When we have little information, a mental image forms regardless, and the brain doesn't know the difference between a stereotype and accurate knowledge and just fills in the blanks. In the example above, while it may be accurate, it's not fair and not always a positive thing. Judgments usually err on the negative side, and thus they are something we want to avoid. How can we avoid being judged by others?

A 1989 study by Hilton and Fein set out to determine the cause of people's judgments, assumptions, and stereotyping. What made the brain immediately assign traits and a veritable backstory to some people versus others? Why were some people so quick to jump to conclusions?

It was found that the less information people had about a certain subject or person, the more they began to fill in the gaps with information that was stereotypical of a general representation. Like with the first example, if you only have a limited set of information, you will fill in the rest with your stereotype of a rich, preppy, affluent WASP with a sweater tied around their neck.

To prevent stereotyping and being instantly judged, Hilary and Fein found that simply providing details about the subject completely unrelated to the stereotype in mind diluted the stereotype and made people more likely to trust and like others. The more detail about the person, the better, even if it was completely random. When we have limited information, we assume a person is just the same as the most stereotypical representation that has those traits.

When we have more information about someone in any regard, we realize we can't define them by those one or two traits, and we cease stereotyping and judging. What does this mean for us? There is no such thing as *too much information* (TMI).

You can make people like you more, stereotype you less, and emotionally invest in you more by providing seemingly useless and nonsensical details about your life. People like to make fun of TMI, but the reality is that TMI can ultimately make you more likable. Of course, preferably you share positive or at least neutral information about yourself.

You become less of a threat and more of a known quantity. People become less suspicious of you and are more willing to give you the benefit of the doubt. By sharing seemingly trivial information about yourself, you allow people to feel like they know you, and they stop making assumptions.

And again, it doesn't even matter if the details are relevant to your identity, career, nonthreatening nature, or life. You can share your preference of glasses brand, your favorite color, and perhaps where you went to school. The more information about you that is out there, the less readily people can judge and stereotype you, simply because you won't fit those stereotypes and assumptions anymore.

For example, what if we learned that the

person who plays tennis and belongs to a country club was poor growing up and went to college on a tennis scholarship? Also, they drive a 20-year old car and prefer to eat burritos. Does that change your view of them? We certainly wouldn't stereotype and make more assumptions about them like we previously did. In fact, the additional information we've learned blows the doors off any category we could put them into. And in a sense, that's the goal: to make it impossible for us to fit into any broad category or generalization. People are only judging you based on what they *aren't* seeing of you.

With more information, people suddenly become three-dimensional and not the static character biographies we see in movies. We are humanized, and we eventually realize that all humans are complex amalgamations. We were never going to fit into a stereotype or box. In reality, you really haven't done anything profound. You haven't even given any information that's important or useful.

Oversharing to maximize likability works to get people to feel that they know different sides of you. An easy way to share more details is to get into the habit of offering unsolicited information. For instance, if someone asks about your weekend, don't resort to answering, "Good, how about yours?" A guideline I like to use is to give four distinct details when answering easy questions—in this way, you will get into the habit of giving people more information, which will make conversation flow better anyway. Here's an example of zero sharing, little information, and a high likelihood of judgment and stereotyping.

Where are you from?
Oklahoma. You?

If you don't know anything about a person besides the fact they are from Oklahoma, where does your mind automatically go? It goes to whatever your stereotypes about Oklahoma are. You don't know if this person was born there, raised there, or only lived there for a couple of years. You don't have the context to make a good judgment about them, and yet you do anyway. This one trait defines them in your mind.

Now, here's an example of why giving unsolicited information can be helpful.

Where are you from?
Oklahoma, but I was born in New York. My parents were originally from France and I grew up visiting France very frequently. Also, I have eight dogs.

Now attempt to put *this* person into a box. It's the same person as before, but it's near-impossible because there is so much information about them that you simply have to take them as they are. By knowing more about them, they have become more humanized and interesting.

The added benefit to sharing unsolicited information and more in general is you make it extremely easy for others to connect with you. When you spout off details about your life, it's easy for them to find common ground and know you as a person. If you divulge personal information or intimate details of your life, you'll also be appearing to take the first steps to building trust and showing vulnerability to others. The more that's out there, the more there is for people to hook onto and relate to.

Let's face it; stereotypes surround us and we judge people every day. In fact, the reason why human beings automatically stereotype and judge each other is that it flows from our survival instincts. Stereotyping lions and lion-shaped creatures was probably helpful to survival.

There is nothing fundamentally wrong with stereotypes, because we use them for convenience and efficiency. However, when we use them to prematurely judge others, it becomes a weakness and a large blow to your likability. Once again, the Pygmalion effect comes into play and we cause people to live up to our expectations of them.

You can defeat judgments people have about

you by oversharing. After all, enough nonsensical detail eventually paints a fairly accurate picture about who you really are.

In 1997, Arthur Aron found that sharing did more than simply make you less susceptible to judgment from others. It creates emotional closeness and investment. In fact, the more intimate and *invasive* the information, the better.

He split participants into two groups. One group questioned each other on 36 very specific and intimate questions, including personal vulnerabilities and insecurities. Sample questions were, "What is your most terrible memory?" and "What is your most treasured memory?" It's impossible to not get personal when faced with these questions. The other group was tasked to ask each other only shallow small-talk questions about their everyday lives.

It's not something people are comfortable doing, but the participants followed directions. We feel like we're offending people or showing too much of ourselves, which is frightening. But the participants who were tasked with asking each other sensitive and sometimes prying personal questions developed greater levels of trust, rapport, and mutual comfort with one another. They felt emotional closeness, even though they didn't know each other before the study.

The other group, however, didn't develop this level of trust, confidence, and intimacy. They essentially remained at their initial level of emotional closeness.

Aron proved that when *you* share information, the *receiving parties* will like you more and feel closer to you and reciprocate. Why does this happen on a practical level?

It's likely that they would feel that you are approachable and easier to relate to. Most of us have issues we are dealing with. Maybe we had traumas in the past. Maybe we are faced with a current challenge that is really frustrating us. While they might not have gone through the exact same things, they can at least empathize with you and feel your pain, confusion, and fear. When you share these personal challenges or struggles, inevitably you will find common ground with others. When you let your guard down, you enable others to empathize with you.

As a general rule, it's better to overshare rather than not share at all. If you're so worried about being looked down upon or being taken advantage of by the person you are speaking with, this will also influence how others perceive you.

Make sure that you share something specific. The starting point is, of course, the basic journalist questions of who, why, what, where, when, and how. You should begin there but not stop there. You should tell people why this experience had such an impact on you. Share real vulnerabilities that involve emotions, fears, insecurities, values, traumatic experiences, and your unconventional way of looking at things.

Don't expect people to share vulnerabilities

with you first. You can, but that would be taking a passive role in being likable. You have to make it happen by taking the first step. Most people will reciprocate because you struck a nerve with them. Once you are exchanging stories, focus on sharing your personal dreams, hopes, aspirations, and emotions.

Share more, share frequently, and overshare. These methods are proven to lead to likability and emotional closeness.

Takeaways:

- A tangent to being likable is not being stereotyped or judged in a negative way. Research has found that judgment comes as a result of incomplete information, so people complete it however they want. If you provide more information about yourself and share, share, share, you will be able to avoid judgment. Therefore, the more information you have present about yourself, no matter how irrelevant it seems, and make yourself a three-dimensional human.

- Sharing as a general policy is good because it makes you more relatable and gives people something to find interesting about you. Sharing and divulging personal details makes people react in an emotional, bonding manner.

Chapter 12. How to Win Groups Over

In previous chapters, we've talked about how to win over individuals.

Many of these lessons apply in different situations, but they tend to work better when you can focus your full attention on one person in particular. In this chapter, I want to talk about how to win groups of people over. We aren't always going to be so fortunate as to be able to focus on one person, and groups are a necessity of life even if you work by yourself. There are fundamentally different dynamics that exist in groups, mainly because you're dealing with a web of relationships, not just the relationship between you and one other person.

What happens when a web of relationships exists? There's herd mentality ("safety in numbers"), mob mentality ("Everyone feels this way? I do too!"), the bystander effect ("Other people are here, so I don't feel any responsibility"), and good old-fashioned follow the leader ("Whatever you say, sir"). Winning groups over consists of calibrating to each of these dynamics when you see them. You don't necessarily have to be the most charismatic and loud person, and you don't even have to be the most popular and well-liked. There are strategic ways to win groups over that capitalize on groupthink, summed up in *social impact theory* (Latane and Wolf, 1981).

Social impact theory proposes that group dynamics and winning a group over are largely a function of three factors:

1. Number: The number of people you want to win over. The fewer, the easier.
2. Immediacy: How close (physically) you are

to everyone in the group, regardless of affiliation. The more immediate, the better.

3. Strength: How important you are to the group in general. The more important you are, the better.

Let's go through each of the three factors.

If you want to win a group over, the smaller the group, the better chance you have. If you are one person and you want to win over 1000 people who are fervently against you, it's likely that you'll be drowned out before you finish your first sentence. However, if you are only trying to convince two people, you are 33% of the people involved. You've got a fighting chance at dealing with two sets of objections over 1000.

If you want to win a group over, the more immediate and tangible you are, the better chance you stand. The more distant you are physically, the more distant you become psychologically. Ask yourself this: why do salespeople always insist on selling in person and setting up appointments rather than conducting business over the phone? Likewise, if you are corresponding with someone over email, you would want to call them to emphasize your point or to really explain yourself. It's natural instinct to do so, because everyone feels they are more convincing the more *immediate* they are.

Finally, if you want to win a group over, the more important to the group you are, the better chance you have. If you are a complete stranger with no sense of credibility and no reason for people to believe you, the group won't care. If you are a stranger with significant credibility, the group will probably care. And if you are a well-known friend with little credibility, the group's level of caring can vary. Obviously, the best way to win a group over is to be perceived as credible and also be liked and known to the group.

There are multiple ways these factors can work with each other. Obviously, the ideal situation for winning the group over would be to maximize all three factors. How can you do this?

For number, you can split the group into smaller groups or factions you can handle one at a time. If your main group is 15 people, set aside time to isolate two to four individuals at a time so you can explain adequately without the herd mentality instantly working against you. Put yourself into a situation where your voice can be easily heard and there is a smaller chance of being teamed up against. Your job might be easier than you think when you consider that most groups tend to unofficially designate one particular member as the leader everyone takes cues from. It happens in social groups just as often as it does office settings.

It's not always conscious; it's just an inevitable dynamic that occurs whenever people gather. Whenever a group tries to decide where to go to dinner, there is always someone who speaks up first and whom others look to for approval and to make the final decision. Isolate this leader who acts as the linchpin for the group and focus your efforts on winning them over. The group will listen to them, and thus you should attempt to get them to listen to you first.

In friend groups, you can spend a lot of time, effort, and resources contacting each individual friend and trying to win them over. That takes too many resources, and at some point, it becomes political when you're running deals behind everyone else's back. Instead, focus on smaller groups in general and the group leader.

To maximize your immediacy and presence to the group, you would want to spend as much time with them as possible, in as close quarters as possible. Frequency of exposure helps as well. Face to face contact is best, with forms of digital communication such as texting or email making barely an impact. Again, you may want to focus more of your in-person attention on the leaders of the group for greatest impact.

Finally, to maximize your importance to the group, you would want to emphasize your credibility and reasons to be listened to, how much people like you and want to simply do you a favor, or the group leader's endorsement of you. To puff up the reasons people should listen to you, you can refer to your official or unofficial credentials and pedigree. Anything that is positive about you and would give implication to intelligence can be referenced. Even if someone has a Ph.D. in an entirely unrelated subject, it will still give you a small amount of credibility.

You can also maximize your importance to the group by playing on the group's emotions and utilizing emotional debt. I'm talking about a guilt trip. Make people feel obligated to listen to you when the only other option is crippling guilt. You likely haven't used it since you were young, but it still works wonders as an adult. Finally, you can even just focus on befriending everyone and becoming important in that aspect.

And once again, if you can work closely together and eventually convince the group leader, the rest of your work might be done for you. They'll endorse you, and you can piggyback off their credibility and importance. Even if you can't directly influence decisions, the group dynamic will be changed in your favor.

Social impact theory also works backward. If these three factors are present, it means *you* will be more easily influenced by a group.

With winning groups over, the greatest overall task isn't necessarily to maximize the factors of social impact theory. It's actually to subvert what's known as *groupthink*, which is the tendency of groups to conform in thought, often to detrimental effects due to the development of blind spots and positive reinforcement. In other words, people in groups think worse and make worse decisions because they are surrounded by an echo chamber of people who only repeat what they hear.

Groupthink was coined by Irving Janis in 1972, and he articulated eight factors that were found in strong instances:

1. Illusion of invulnerability: Together we can't all be wrong, they can't get all of us, and there's strength in numbers.

2. Collective rationalization: This all looks correct, right? No one is saying anything negative about it. If so many of us agree, we must be right.

3. Belief in inherent morality: We are all correct, and everyone else is wrong. Therefore, we have carte blanche to act in our moral superiority.

4. Stereotyped views of people outside the group: They have no idea what they're talking about, and they are all stupid anyway. Let's stick together.

5. Direct pressure on dissenters: Don't you dare bring up your negative arguments. I won't tell anyone, but people are going to get so mad at you if you tell them!

6. Self-censorship: I'll just keep this to myself. I don't want to upset people or get on people's bad sides. I'm probably wrong, anyway.

7. Illusion of unanimity: I think everyone in the group, 100% of us, think this, right?

Right.

8. Self-appointed "mindguards": Avoid the newspapers today, everyone. The views expressed are out of context and borderline lies. They don't know what we are doing. Only we do. Don't listen to outside sources, and protect yourselves from their influence.

No matter how smart your decision or argument is, if you go against a well-founded, deep groupthink, you're going to be in trouble. This is how cults form and how people become radicalized to terrorist groups.

Any and all arguments quickly become about defending the group versus having actual discourse. Most of the time in this book, we can use that for good. If you feel comfortable, you can even use elements of groupthink to win over a group in conjunction with the first three factors. But it's easy to see how it can be used for nefarious purposes by preying on people's desire to belong and feel validation.

Takeaways:

- Winning over groups is a bit more complex and involved than winning over individuals. With individuals, you can focus your full attention and unleash tips from other chapters in this book.
- With groups, you have to focus on three main factors: how important you are to the group, the size of the group, and how tangible your presence is.
- An additional means of winning over a group is groupthink, but that can verge into cult psychology and clearly encourages an "us versus them" perspective.

Chapter 13. How to Be Funny and Charismatic

Much of what has been presented in this book thus far may not be surprising to you. For some, these techniques might be helpful reminders, and for others, they might be mere extensions of what you already know.

Many of the tips might be intuitive, and even obvious, in hindsight. There are many aspects of human interaction that we pick up just from being a functioning member of society, like basic manners or tucking in your shirt when you want to appear more tidy and clean. It's not until they are pointed out that they become clear, but nonetheless, the art of being charming isn't necessarily rocket science.

Thus, in this chapter, I want to take the opportunity to present two studies about what truly makes people likable and charismatic. These might not be so obvious in hindsight, and they have been proven and confirmed with scientific rigor. Remember, despite what you might think, the evidence says otherwise.

Quicker Is Better

The first study is titled "Quick Thinkers Are Smooth Talkers: Mental Speed Facilitates Charisma" and was conducted by William von Hippel in 2015. As you might gather from the name, his discovery was that speed of thought and dialogue was more related to people's ratings of charisma than many other traits, including being correct or accurate. In fact, if you were to prioritize one aspect of interaction, quickness would be highest rated.

The researchers asked test participants to rate how quick-witted, funny, or charismatic their friends were depending on how they performed on a series of tests. Friends of the participants were also present and observing the tests. In the first test, participants were asked to answer trivia questions given out in rapid succession. Afterward, the participants' friends were asked to rate their friends who actually took the tests.

Conventionally, you would think that the friends of the participants would rate their friend as more charismatic, quick-witted, or funny depending on how frequently they answered correctly in the first test. That was not the case whatsoever. It turns out charisma wasn't related to accuracy or even the appearance of intelligence.

What mattered most was how quickly the participants answered—the speed with which they took action. Keeping in mind the parameters of the experiment didn't specify a right answer, the friends of the participants didn't necessarily care whether the participant performed the task correctly. All they based their decisions on was how quickly they answered.

The researchers concluded that people tend to have a more favorable impression of you depending on how quickly you speak or take a position. It doesn't really matter whether you are correct in your position. People tend to have a natural attraction to others who "think on their feet," and the accuracy of your statements doesn't matter as much as how quick and sharp you seem to other people. The implication is that speed is associated with intelligence and social acumen. We feel amazing when we can get a dig in at someone at just the right moment instead of thinking of it two hours later while showering. It might also feel that people are better listeners if they respond quickly to you, albeit in an incorrect way.

So to appear more charismatic, it's clearly better to speak first and loudly, even if you have nothing to say and even if you are speaking gibberish. Slow and silent, while it may not be seen as negative, clearly won't have the overwhelming positive effect that acting quickly will have.

At the outset, this seems absurd, because the study seems to suggest that talking out of your behind, as long as it is quick and confident, will make you more likable. Then again, is it actually so surprising? Humans place incredible weight on *perception*.

When someone replies to a question or provides an opinion or stance quickly, we assume they are confident and knowledgeable—because only those types of people would move quickly. So because we assume that people will only speak quickly if they have something valuable to say, if someone speaks quickly, we assume it's valuable. In other words, if X, then Y, where X is knowledge or confidence and Y is speed. Moreover, if someone replies slowly, we naturally start to assume the opposite—their brain processing speed is lower, and they have nothing valuable to add.

The study confirms that we think *if Y, then X*. Of course, this is wrong and it's not cause or even causation, but we can use this knowledge to our advantage.

Speak first and speak quickly. You can always correct what you said after the fact. What's important is that you were able to say something quickly when prompted. When you're talking to people, make it your priority to respond in any way possible. Silences and lulls are your worst enemy. In many cases, the person probably won't care whether you have the right answer or not; they just want some type of answer or response.

If you're overly concerned with giving a correct, accurate, or even perfect response, your charisma quotient will drop if it's done slowly. This is the same approach that will cause a singer to work on a song for two weeks, singing the same line in slightly different ways, while another singer will spend the same time producing eight songs. That's simply not the currency that matters in likability.

For instance, if you meet somebody at a party and they're talking about a problem they have at work, they don't expect you to actually solve their problem. They put it out there for the sake of conversation. If you respond to the information they shared by digesting it slowly, turning it many times in your mind and cross-referencing it with your past experiences, it may take you a painfully long time to answer. By that time, the conversation has probably taken many different turns or will be well on its way to ending.

A quick *anything* is better than a slow monologue. After all, isn't that what we see in movies and television shows—flowing banter that is quick like a ping-pong match? You might have to fight your mental programming to not speak in platitudes or speak just to make noise, but you should in pursuit of charisma.

Speak first, and you can always backtrack afterward and correct yourself: "Let me rephrase that," or "Going back to what I said, I have a different approach."

You can also speak first, think through your thoughts out loud, and find your way as you are speaking: "Well, see, that's an interesting point. What do I think about it? Good question. Here's what I think. It might be good, but it could also be bad because…"

What's important is to maintain the momentum of the conversation. Keep that tempo, pace, and rhythm going by filling the silence and thinking quickly to be perceived as charismatic. A thoughtful response in a brief window of time is less important than you'd think, and mental speed is far more valued. Humans are emotional beings, and speed and confidence of presentation are always going to elicit a stronger emotional response than a well-thought-out answer.

An easy way to be quicker is to practice *free association*. Open any book and blindly put your finger on a page. What word did your finger point to? Now, as quickly as possible, think of five words, things, people, places, concepts, or thoughts the word makes you think of—without filtering. Then repeat the process with another word. The ability to pivot from topic to related topic is the backbone of flowing conversation. Your speed of thought will increase greatly, and you'll be a verbal ping-pong master when you improve at free association.

The researcher Von Hippel perhaps summed it up best: "Although we expected mental speed to predict charisma, we thought that it would be less important than IQ. Instead, we found that how smart people were was less important than how quick they were."

Benign Moral Violations Are Funny

The second study is about exactly what we find funny and why. It turns out there is a science to what some might call crude humor—it functions on a principle called *benign moral violations,* which is something proposed in the 2010 research paper "Benign Violations: Making Immoral Behavior Funny" by professor Peter McGraw at the University of Colorado Boulder.

Humor is mostly seen as subjective, and we can see this to be partially true as humor does not tend to translate across cultural lines. For instance, there are no comedy movies that have consistently struck gold in international box offices because humor is rooted in language and contextual norms. However, action and adventure movies routinely break box office records because there's no cultural translation required for an explosion or flying car.

We can see that humor is usually unreliable, and you can't assume that, just because you find something funny, other people will even smile. Understandably, this makes it difficult to be charming and likable because however funny one person might find you, you could very well be insulting and nonsensical to another.

However, according to McGraw, there is one approach to humor that is fairly universal and consistent. Regardless of whom you're with, the culture you're in, or the social context you find yourself in, you can always draw on the power of the benign moral violation.

Researchers asked participants about hypothetical situations that breached a widely recognized social norm, such as farting in public or spilling a drink all over your supervisor. The researchers only asked two questions:

1. Was the behavior *immoral or wrong* to some degree?
2. Was it funny?

There was a very high correlation between the two—meaning the more immoral the behavior, the funnier it was rated.

However, if the behavior was too immoral, then it quickly became unfunny and verged into cruel territory. This is where the researchers coined the term "benign moral violation"—the act needs to be immoral, but in a way that appears harmless or distant and has no negative repercussions. To be truly benign, the violation should be purely amusing, inoffensive, and psychologically distant, which means it doesn't appear real or tangible. We can laugh at others, but not if they are *really* suffering.

Other examples include:

1. Someone falling over and their pants coming off in the process
2. A ball hitting someone in the crotch
3. Making a gaffe when meeting someone famous or important

See how these are a bit crass and *wrong* but ultimately harmless because nothing is hurt besides people's sense of pride? Toilet humor is universal, and now we perhaps understand why! Overall, this study tells us we shouldn't be too afraid of *going there* when talking to other people.

You may have come across the advice that you should stray from talking about religion, sex, and politics, but in some cases, if we find them as theoretical, hypothetical, and otherwise distant, what we say about them can come off as funny. It really all boils down to whether the moral violation involved in this story is benign or outrageous. If it's silly and outrageous, it's benign, and you've got a good chance of tackling tough topics. However, if it hits too close to home and becomes serious, then it's not benign and just becomes plain offensive.

What makes a violation funny is people are openly talking about something they have been trained not to—just a little bit over the line while not completely obliterating it. The tricky part is to know just how far you can push the envelope.

Without a proper sense of social calibration, it wouldn't be difficult to overdo things and focus so much on the shock value that you achieve the complete opposite effect. Instead of people finding you funny with an interesting sense of humor, they would instantly dismiss you as an overstepping ass.

Additionally, your moral violation can't be too benign, otherwise it will be run of the mill and boring. On the other hand, your moral violation can't be too great of a violation, otherwise people will be supremely uncomfortable and even emotionally affected. It's a quite a tightrope to walk. Unfortunately, if you don't practice this, it's too easy to make the wrong call.

Make people laugh with the violation, but keep them comfortable because it's benign. If someone falls on their face in front of you, there will be initial shock and worry. But if you discover they tripped by stepping on a banana and they are 100% fine, then you are going to find this situation funny because, hey, it is.

Closely related to this idea of the benign moral violation is the German concept of *schadenfreude*, which is defined as finding pleasure or amusement in someone else's suffering. It's only mean-spirited and in poor taste if we laugh when someone is truly hurt, but to laugh when someone has been violated in a benign way is very natural and widespread.

The underlying point is it's not negative to talk about negative things. You can bring up negative topics, moral violations or whatnot without turning your conversation sour. You might even be seen as hilarious. There's a line, but it might not be as thin as you think it is. This is also similar to the advice in an earlier chapter to act the part of a friend and thus be welcomed as one. Friends laugh at each other and make off-color, silly, infantile jokes; this is just another dimension of not treating someone like a stranger and thus setting the tone for friendship.

The conclusions from these two studies may not be immediately obvious in hindsight, but they are certainly behaviors we can incorporate into our interactions to be more likable.

Takeaways:

- Studies have shown that accuracy or even logic is not charismatic or likable in some instances. Instead, speed of response and wit is key. It doesn't matter what you say, just as long as you say something quickly. People are emotion and perception-driven, and quickness activates those. Unfortunately, this is a habit very few of us possess, so an exercise to assist with this is free association.

- Another study has shown that the root of what is funny is, surprisingly or not, toilet humor. It was posited that most humor can be defined by a benign moral violation—something that is wrong to laugh at but harmless overall. This is another aspect of not treating people like strangers and thus setting the tone of friendship.

Chapter 14. How to Chit-Chat Effectively

In other words, gossip. How do you gossip effectively? What does that even mean?

When we think about gossip, we think about mean teenage girls whispering to each other, pointing at someone, and then laughing. That's certainly one version of it, and sometimes, adults aren't much better.

Gossiping is when you talk about other people behind their back, but it doesn't necessarily have to be in a negative light. It's just talking about relationships, connections, and who is doing what. You don't have to talk about the adulterous relationships or scandalous connections. The truth is that the act of gossiping is a highly pro-social and bonding activity, and it doesn't have to be nefarious in nature.

If Jane got a new job, you can focus on how happy you are for her and how spacious her new office will be instead of snickering about how lucky she was and how you would never hire her. Of course, that might be the less interesting conversation.

You can also choose to simply abstain from talking about these matters and calmly state, "I don't like to gossip about people behind their backs" in an attempt to take the moral high road and hope that people follow you. Whatever the case, and whatever the approach you want to take, realize that engaging in gossip and what appears to be idle chit-chat can cement a relationship.

In 1998, behavioral psychologist Robin Dunbar put forth a theory about human relationships she made after observing chimpanzees. Chimpanzees are one species of many mammals that engage in what is known as *social grooming*. You know this to be when chimpanzees pick the bugs out of each other's fur and eat them. You also know this to be when your mother used to fix your hair and arrange your shirt collars just as you were about to leave.

Social grooming increases the amount of stability and cohesion in any given group, and it has also been found to be indicative of social structure and hierarchies, with alpha males receiving more grooming. This grooming ritual cements social bonds. It also ensures that everybody has their place in the social hierarchy. It's a form of social lubrication that maintains harmony among chimpanzees. It is how chimps become familiar and comfortable with each other and how trust is created.

Humans haven't needed to engage in social grooming for many years, but Dunbar proposed that to replace the stabilizing effects of social grooming, humans instead gossip and chit-chat about others. Gossip helps us relate to others and maintain relationships in the same way social grooming does for chimpanzees. It fills the same gap for what we do when we are sitting idly with nothing in particular to do but pass the time.

Gossip can serve a purpose, such as discussing important matters of food, shelter, and the well-being of the group or tribe. It can also serve no purpose at all and simply act to familiarize people with each other. It doesn't have to be negative or positive in nature; it just has to fill the air. An additional part of Dunbar's theory is that language allowed us to gossip and exchange information. Whatever the case, relationships are being formed and cemented on the basis of something we tend to overlook or downplay as negative—simple gossip and chit-chat.

What does this mean for us? Is it as simple as being willing to engage in gossip more frequently?

Sort of. What we downplay as gossip can

actually be the basis for forming relationships. Gossip always has the option of leading somewhere large and intimate, no matter how small it can start. It also doesn't necessarily have to be negative in nature, and even if it is, it will still help you bond. Talk about social relationships in particular. This really lends support to the conclusion that talking in general, about people, yourself, or anything at all, allows people to know you and like you. When you engage with people about idle chit-chat and discuss people, relationships, and shared situations, that's what leads to bonding.

Yes, that even includes banal, boring small talk. That can certainly be classified as gossip, and while you may hate it, there is no reason for small talk to remain small, vague, and uninteresting.

Allow yourself to be exposed and open to other people. Ask questions and divulge information about yourself, just like you learned in earlier chapters on how to treat people like friends and break stereotyping.

Establish a mutual level of comfort and familiarity. If nothing else, it gets people to drop their guard.

Another 1998 study harped on the importance of staying positive with gossip (Skowronski, J. J., Carlston, D. E., Mae, L., & Crawford).

In the experiment, researchers asked actors to read a script where they would describe other people. These scripts varied from pleasant and positive to downright negative and nasty. Other participants would then pay attention to the person reading and give their assessment as to that person's likability.

The research results were quite astonishing. It turned out that the people observing the reader transferred the traits that the person was describing to the reader. For example, if the reader characterized someone as nasty, insensitive, arrogant, or rude, the other people in the study observing the reader reported that the actor exhibited those same traits. Similarly, when the reader was tasked to read the script where they would describe the other person in glowing terms, the bystanders would likewise report that the reader was positive, cheerful, and bubbly.

If you're not talking about yourself, people will make judgments about you based on how you describe other people. They equate how you read other people with your own personality traits. If you ever find yourself in a conversation and the flow of the talk veers toward talking about third parties, keep this study in mind.

Gossipers, pay attention. You don't even have to come off as nasty—the people you're talking to just focus on your words. This is why It Is really Important to watch how you describe other people. Words really matter.

The way you choose to talk about others can impact the perception of the person you're speaking to because of *spontaneous trait transference*. Whatever traits you describe in others, people will transfer to you. If you talk about someone being lazy, people will more likely think you're lazy. If you describe others as engaging and cheerful, they will also think that about you. Obviously, to make this work best for you, you should only describe others as positive, encouraging, and overall likable people, even if you're talking about somebody who's downright unpleasant. There are still some pleasant parts to that person's personality or life story you can choose to dwell on.

You can even choose better words. Instead of describing someone as fat and bloated, describing them as a little bigger or round has a positive impact on how people will perceive you. The way you choose your words packs a lot of value and judgment. Not only are you judging people with your words, but your word choice also says a lot about you.

Don't let your comfort level guide you. Some people really feel comfortable talking negatively. Instead, pay attention to the words you are using. If you can't say anything positive, then at least try to say something neutral. If you feel that that won't work, try to hold off on saying anything at all. If you wish to be proactive about how people perceive you, try to be as positive as possible. Compliment others behind their backs. Try to find the silver lining of the dark cloud when describing negative situations. Tell stories about how great or interesting people are and make them the heroes of your stories.

Overall, to chit-chat more effectively, don't be afraid to open up and gossip—but make sure to err on the positive, otherwise people will think you're whatever evil you are describing.

Takeaways:

- Social grooming is something that chimps do, but humans also have a version in gossip. Both are where bonds are made and where likability is created. The lesson is to engage in what you feel is gossip— talking about people, situations, social contexts, and local events. Gossip doesn't have to be negative; it just has to be something where discussion is made.

- To reiterate, gossip doesn't have to be negative. In fact, it shouldn't, otherwise you may fall prey to spontaneous trait transference, which is when people start to associate you with the traits you describe in others.

Conclusion

Looks like my psychology degree has paid off! No, the jury is still out on that one, but it's certainly helped me learn how to become more likable and charming in my own life.

But it's not like I ask everyone what we have in common when I first meet them or purposefully trip over curbs to appear vulnerable and likable. Nor do I constantly ask people what they did that day or provide nonsensical information about myself to avoid stereotyping.

That wouldn't the best way to use the knowledge in this book.

Just as the way these psychological phenomena subconsciously affect others, you should invoke them subtly and subconsciously as well. The effects aren't something that you are going to be able to quantify immediately, but little by little, your life will begin to change.

The science of likability is how you can use empirical studies and evidence to make people like you. Even if you don't trust yourself, your intuition, or other people's advice, rest assured that the weight of evidence and proof is on your side.

That's the beauty of the scientific method!

Sincerely,

Patrick King
Social Interaction Specialist and Conversation Coach
www.PatrickKingConsulting.com

P.S. If you enjoyed this book, please don't be shy and drop me a line, leave a review, or both! I love reading feedback, and reviews are the lifeblood of Kindle books, so they are always welcome and greatly appreciated.

Speaking and Coaching

Imagine going far beyond the contents of this book and dramatically improving the way you interact with the world, as well as the relationships you'll build.

Are you interested in contacting Patrick for...

- ... a social skills workshop for your workplace?
- ... speaking engagements on the power of conversation and charisma?
- ... personalized social skills and conversation coaching?

Patrick speaks around the world to help

people improve their lives through the power of building relationships with improved social skills. He is a recognized industry expert, bestselling author, and speaker.

To invite Patrick to speak at your next event or to inquire about coaching, get in touch directly through his website's contact form at http://www.PatrickKingConsulting.com/contact or contact him directly at Patrick@patrickkingconsulting.com.

Cheat Sheet

Chapter 1. How to Improve People's Moods

- Most people tend to rely on luck or happenstance to strike up friendships and be likable. This is the wrong approach because It undermines your own abilities. One of the ways we can make friends more easily and have better impressions is by improving people's moods.
- Improving people's moods involves invoking times they were already in a good mood from their memory banks, because memory is heavily context-dependent. As an added bonus, once you are able to

create a good mood in others, you yourself become part of those memories, and they are positively conditioned to enjoy your presence.

- Other ways to improve people's moods include positivity, generating goodwill, and associating yourself with things people like and enjoy. Compliments are another easy way to do this on a daily basis.

Chapter 2. How to Turn Enemies into Friends

- You might be the friendliest and most benign person in the world, and still you will offend someone. That's just the reality of life, but you don't have to take it lying down.

- An easy way to turn an enemy into a friend is with the Benjamin Franklin effect, where you invoke cognitive dissonance by asking an enemy to perform a small favor for you. They will justify to themselves that you are not so bad after all if they performed a favor for you. In addition, you are initiating contact, which tends to humanize others.

- A final way to turn an enemy into a friend

is to perform favors for them. This is more intuitive and easily understood—if you present value to someone, they will like you more. Or at least, they won't consider you completely useless, and that's the best we can do with some people. The goal is to blur the lines people have created in their minds and make it easier to be accepted.

Chapter 3. How to Create the Foundation of Friendship

- Equity and feelings of fairness play a large part in the foundation of friendship. That is to say, people don't like the negative feelings associated with either side of unfairness. They don't like feeling like they are being used, nor do they like feeling like they are cheating someone. Therefore, emphasize fair play and equity in terms of the value (which is subjective and can vary widely) you are putting into a relationship or friendship.
- Similarity is another large aspect of the foundation of friendship. We like those who are similar to ourselves instinctively.

These days, we take similarity to mean a higher chance of bonding and matching worldviews and positive traits.

- Humans are more similar to each other than not. We all bleed and put our pants on one leg at a time. Therefore, it is up to you to either search for or create similarities. You can *search* for similarities by becoming comfortable with questions and the feeling that you are being slightly invasive, and you can *create* similarities using the psychological phenomenon of mirroring.

Chapter 4. How to Act the Part

- Often, we treat people like strangers when we meet them. This sounds natural, but it is actually detrimental to building rapport and being likable. Treat them like a friend and they will treat you like a friend. This is backed up by the theory of transference, which states that people transfer their emotions of someone else to those they see acting in a familiar way or role.
- We don't realize it, but we have the ability to set the tone of our relationships, and

you might be causing the very source of your unhappiness by not acting the part of a friend.

- Another aspect of treating people like a friend right off the bat is to understand how the Pygmalion effect works. People live up to the expectations we give them. If we treat them like strangers, they will remain strangers. If we expect that they are interesting, we will treat them in a way that allows them to demonstrate this. All of this requires more effort on your part, but you have the ability to set the tone, so use it.

Chapter 5. How to Persuade and Negotiate Effectively

- Negotiation is difficult, but that's mostly If you are only negotiating on one plane and not realizing that people have desires you can help fulfill. One of the keys of good negotiation is not only getting a good price, but also making both parties feel happy about getting some type of win.
- The foot in the door technique is helpful because you get to capitalize on people's

tendency to drain willpower when they start with saying yes.

- The door in the face technique operates on the opposite principle—once you ask for something huge initially, anything else you ask for will be deemed reasonable.

Chapter 6. How to Gain Trust and Credibility

- Trust has been shown to work on a linear fashion. The more you see someone, the more you trust them, regardless of interaction or depth. This is known as the Propinquity effect, and it is similar to how studies have shown that customers only purchase after seeing a product seven times. It is also similar to the mere exposure effect.
- Credibility is a notch above trust, and there are also proven ways to generate that feeling. These include highlighting qualifications, showing your caring, showing similarity, being assertive, showing social proof, not contradicting yourself, and avoiding being overly polite.

Chapter 7. How to Work Well With Others

- The stimulus-value-role model of social interaction states that to get to someone's inner circle, you have to show three levels of compatibility: stimulus, value, and role. To use this model, you have to first understand which stage you are currently at with someone, and then you can understand what you need to get into the next stage. The deepest level is role: working together, collaborating, and resolving conflict.

- Within working together successfully, there is a gender divide where males are more comfortable with competition and comparison. However, no matter who you are working with, people will favor you if you can make them feel good about themselves.

Chapter 8. How to Be More Endearing

- One of the easiest ways to be endearing is to stop trying to be perfect and impressive. Instead, try to be relatable and harmless to a degree. Nothing epitomizes that better than the Pratfall effect, which shows the attractiveness of imperfection and vulnerability. This also works because you are catering to people's insecurities and allowing them to feel that judgment is not imminent.

- Another aspect of being endearing is to make rough times better, which is possible through using the Losada ratio. This ratio should govern the amount of positive and negative remarks you use—roughly five positive to make up for one negative.

- Finally, you can be endearing if you make other people feel like experts and ask them questions they feel they are specially equipped to answer.

Chapter 9. How to Convince People To Act

- Reverse psychology works on children, and the slightly more advanced form, reactance theory, works on adults. Reactance theory is when you can subtly push people in a direction you want because they feel that you are trying to restrict their free will regarding it.

- The important factor is that someone

feels like they are being restricted in a way that is unfair and arbitrary, which leads to psychological discomfort.

Chapter 10. How to Lead Anyone

- There are six types of leadership, and it's up to you to discover which suits you best and is most effective in your context.
- Visionary: "Come with me to a better world."
- Coaching: "Try this, and you might learn from it."
- Affiliate: "Only If everyone feels good about it."
- Democratic: "What does everyone think?"
- Pace-setting: "Do more faster."
- Commanding: "Do what I say."

Chapter 11. How to Avoid Being Judged

- A tangent to being likable is not being stereotyped or judged in a negative way. Research has found that judgment comes as a result of incomplete information, so people complete it however they want. If you provide more information about yourself and share, share, share, you will be able to avoid judgment. Therefore, the more information you have present about yourself, no matter how irrelevant it seems, and make yourself a three-dimensional human.

- Sharing as a general policy is good because it makes you more relatable and gives people something to find interesting about you. Sharing and divulging personal details makes people react in an emotional, bonding manner.

Chapter 12. How to Win Groups Over

- Winning over groups is a bit more complex and involved than winning over individuals. With individuals, you can focus your full attention and unleash tips from other chapters in this book.
- With groups, you have to focus on three main factors: how important you are to the group, the size of the group, and how tangible your presence is.
- An additional means of winning over a group is groupthink, but that can verge into cult psychology and clearly

encourages an "us versus them" perspective.

Chapter 13. How to Be Funny and Charismatic

- Studies have shown that accuracy or even logic is not charismatic or likable in some instances. Instead, speed of response and wit is key. It doesn't matter what you say, just as long as you say something quickly. People are emotion and perception-driven, and quickness activates those. Unfortunately, this is a habit very few of us possess, so an exercise to assist with this is free association.

- Another study has shown that the root of what is funny is, surprisingly or not, toilet humor. It was posited that most humor can be defined by a benign moral violation—something that is wrong to laugh at but harmless overall. This is another aspect of not treating people like strangers and thus setting the tone of friendship.

Chapter 14. How to Chit-Chat Effectively

- Social grooming is something that chimps do, but humans also have a version in gossip. Both are where bonds are made and where likability is created. The lesson is to engage in what you feel is gossip—talking about people, situations, social contexts, and local events. Gossip doesn't have to be negative; it just has to be something where discussion is made.

- To reiterate, gossip doesn't have to be negative. In fact, it shouldn't, otherwise you may fall prey to spontaneous trait transference, which is when people start to associate you with the traits you describe in others.

Made in the USA
Columbia, SC
25 March 2018